PROJECT SAVE COLLEGIATE ATHLETES

PROJECT SAVE COLLEGIATE ATHLETES

RYAN ALU

Idealism Towers Company

CONTENTS

CHAPTER 1

The Purpose

I have a strong distaste for self-help books, yet here I am, writing precisely that. Self-help books are largely un-Socratic where the author fully believes his teachings are correct and the reader simply has to follow them to lead a more fulfilling life. I want to avoid this arrogance as an author by encouraging you, the reader, to analyze my writing with intense skepticism. I am not a licensed therapist or psychologist, but my journey as an athlete has shaped my philosophies and how I play my sport, volleyball. Even though my experience is through a volleyball lens, I believe the philosophies and teachings in this book are applicable to all collegiate athletes of all sports. My philosophies may or may not help you, but I believe reading accounts of a fellow athlete who has taken on similar challenges you might be facing is always beneficial.

It is important to understand what has compelled me to write this book so you can better understand my intentions and messages. I believe there is a collective emotional and mental suffering among many collegiate athletes due to the lack of preparation and guidance to take on the taxing battle of being a college athlete.

As a collegiate athlete, from 2017 to 2020, I struggled immensely. My expectations of playing for my college were vastly different from the reality, and upon completing my time at the school I was left with bittersweet feelings. I was glad I completed the journey and felt like I had grown as a person; however, I did not feel like I enjoyed it. After graduating, I went on to earn my master's degree at Dartmouth College. At Dartmouth, I found myself in a unique position. Due to the love I had for volleyball and a coach who needed extra players at practice, I ended up becoming a practice player for the Dartmouth Women's Varsity Team. To my surprise, I watched unfold some of the exact same problems, complaints, dramas, and beliefs expressed by the girls that I had during my undergrad experience. Some of the conversations about complaints with the coach, feelings of stagnancy, and overall unfulfillment were so similar I felt deja-vu. The girls were living out the same life I had just finished.

I was in a position where I could help, and I felt obligated to at least try to give guidance. As I attempted to offer wisdom to the girls, I realized the best way to help would be to package all of my ideas into a guidebook.

This is that guidebook.

CHAPTER 2

The Origin Story

I have addressed why I felt compelled to write this book. I shall now address where my philosophies originated. It has been said that the best progress comes out of hardship. In my case, the hardship was my collegiate athletic experience, and the progress was the development of my philosophies. Allow me to tell the story of my battle as a Division I athlete at Ship Weight University (name changed for privacy and to not detract from the original intent of the book).

Before you read the story, I want you to understand that the intent behind explaining my experience is to perfectly capture who I was at the time. My goal is to accurately portray my thoughts, emotions, beliefs, and ideology during my time at Ship Weight. Hopefully, as a fellow collegiate athlete, you will relate to a lot of my logic and feelings at the time. The person that I am about to capture with my writing, the old me from ages 18-21, is not the same person I am now. The old Ryan had flawed logic, an incorrect perception of collegiate athletics, and was grossly unprepared for what he signed up for. So, this is not a book about vengeance, it is not a book about bitterness, it is not a book about trying to show off, and it is not a book about trying to prove that I deserved more. Read the story and see if you relate to old Ryan. Later in the book, we will show why old Ryan was wrong in a lot of ways, allowing you to use his journey as a guide to obtaining a better collegiate athletic experience.

Let us commence.

I have been playing volleyball my entire life. I grew up in a volleyball family and started playing at a very young age. When I was 14 years old I was selected by USA Volleyball to play on the Future Select National Team. The team was comprised of just 12 kids chosen from tryouts all over the country. I remained in the USA Volleyball pipeline until I was 17 years old and I believed I was one of the better liberos in the country. Around this time, since I excelled in the sport, I started dreaming to play at the Division I level. Around recruiting time, my sophomore year of high school, I published my highlight videos and contacted many Division I schools.

To my surprise, slowly but surely, I was consistently rejected. I was third on the list at IPFW. I was told I was a "tier three libero" by George Mason. I was outcasted by UC Irvine after they found out I was from the east coast. Many schools didn't answer. My last remaining hope was Princeton where the coach told me I could walk on if I got past the admissions office. It all changed when Coach Billy (name changed for privacy and to not detract from the original intent of the book) at Ship Weight University called me late into my senior year and told me that I had a Division I spot on his team. I was ecstatic. I was later rejected by Princeton and told Coach Billy that I was going to Ship Weight. Little did I know, I signed up for one of the most emotionally and mentally difficult challenges of my life.

MY FIRST YEAR

Upon arriving at Ship Weight, I knew immediately the culture on the volleyball team was nothing short of toxic. The team was founded on crippling ideologies of seniority, hazing, bullying, ostracizing, and groupthink. Some hazing was not that intense. For example, as freshmen, we were told that the team dressed up for away games. When we arrived at the bus to travel to our first away game, we were the only ones dressed up. Other hazing was more intense. For freshmen to be initiated into the team, we had to allow the upperclassmen to urinate on us in the shower. In addition to these rituals, freshmen had the responsibilities of filling up the water, setting up all the nets, and doing any other chores that no one felt like completing.

After being fooled into dressing up for the first away game, I was disappointed and angry with the team culture. I went to Coach Billy to express my frustrations and told him about the hazing and toxic seniority on the team. I even mentioned other cynical traditions such as the team roast, where the freshmen were forced to make a roast about every single player on the team. This got ugly fast as certain players would give the freshmen roast lines to secretly go after other teammates. I told him that I refused to shower with the team because I had no trust in them and I wanted to hear his thoughts on the current condition of the team culture.

Coach Billy expressed equal disappointment with the culture and knew about several of the traditions. He told me that he needed my help to turn the culture around on the team. In order to do this, he encouraged me to stand up to the seniors and not play into the seniority and hazing. He knew this would cause contention at first but ensured me that he would support me and defend me in every altercation. I agreed to the idea and embarked on a mission to slowly try to change the culture of the team for the better.

So, I stood up to the upperclassmen, who made up the majority of the team, and protested seniority. When they told me to shower with them so they could "initiate me," I told them no. I calmly informed them that I would only shower after all the upperclassmen left. When they told me to set up the net, I told them that I would only do it if they helped me. If they yelled at me to bring the water to the gym, I would tell them I'd only do it if one of the upperclassmen brought it back. I challenged them every step of the way and resisted every bit of seniority.

This naturally led the upperclassmen to despise me. I wouldn't play their game and they HATED it.

But the upperclassmen's hatred for me did not really affect the grand scheme of volleyball. I was not starting as a freshman because an older player, Kevin (name changed for privacy and to not detract from the original intent of the book), was destined to start. The upperclassmen and I tolerated each other. They would say mean things and bully me. I would refuse to be treated as a subordinate. Life went on.

Things changed when Kevin and three other upperclassmen were suspended for the entire season days before our first match. Our first game was in California, and our flight left in three days. I was now thrust into the starting role.

We flew out to California and the tension between the remaining upperclassmen and me lingered, but we managed to ignore our feud for the games and acted civil on the court. We played well as a team and were happy with our trip, finishing 2-2 with two upset wins over Stanford and UC Santa Barbara.

Upon returning we forwent rest and had practice the next day. Our team was the only team on campus, and all food venues were shut down. In order to feed the team, Coach Billy bought everyone sandwiches from a restaurant in town and had them delivered to the gym. I asked my friend on the team if he could pick up my sandwich, since I was the furthest from the gym, and he obliged.

About ten minutes later, as I was sitting in the lobby of my dorm building, I received a knock at the front door. It was not my friend but one of the upperclassmen with my sandwich. I thought this was suspicious since we did not really like each other, but maybe this was a peace offering since the team had done so well in California. I opened the door and he immediately grabbed my arm. I instinctively yanked away in surprise but he had my sleeve and arm pinned. He was trying to pull me outside but I managed to lean back hard enough to remain inside. I was unsure of his intentions. Was this a joke? Was he being playful? The struggle continued as I fought with all of my might to break free from his grasp. Three other upperclassmen jumped out from the sides of the building, rushed in, and grabbed me. I had no chance as it was now a four-against-one attack. They carried me outside as I was writhing, trying to break free, and threw me onto the ice. I landed hard on my back, my phone went flying, and my attackers fled and drove off laughing. I was now covered in snow, my phone was soaked, and my sandwich was soggy as it was tossed in the snow in front of me. I didn't really know what to do. I gathered myself, went inside, changed clothes, and threw my sandwich out. I then went to the team lift to work out with the same people who just jumped me.

Confused, ashamed, embarrassed, and angry, I went to Coach Billy after the team lift and informed him of what had just happened to me. I expected Coach Billy to punish these players. I wanted him to kick them off of the team and discipline them in some way. I was requesting the support that he promised me at the beginning of the season. I was astonished to hear his response. He told me that although their way of handling the situation was poor, they had a point with what they were trying to say with their actions. He continued and told me that I should not have been lazy, should have gotten the sandwich myself, and although they should not have jumped me, their anger toward me was justified, and they were just trying to teach me a lesson.

Eighteen-year-old me did not really know how to handle this. How do I tell my parents that I was just attacked? How do I tell my parents that my coach was not going to protect me? I did not know what to do.

But I did not want to give up. I knew I loved volleyball, and I knew I had a game the following weekend, so I decided to stay as far away from the upperclassmen as possible and just keep playing my game. I would no longer go into the locker room and would change underneath the stairwell outside the gym for several weeks until things cooled down. I wouldn't walk to practice with anyone and wouldn't walk out of practice with anyone. I stopped eating with the team. I just wanted to focus on playing and avoid all of the hatred.

A couple of days after the incident, I was called into Coach Billy's office. He sat me down and told me that I would not start for the upcoming match. Considering I had been playing well and just came back from a successful trip to California, I was confused by the sudden change. Coach Billy informed me that since I did not get along with the team, he could not start me. He went from encouraging me to change the culture of the team for the better, to completely abandoning me and siding with my attackers. I was destroyed. I asked him what had changed in the previous few days to make this decision. The upperclassmen and I had never gotten along because of the battle to control the culture. Why could I start in California but not now? Coach Billy told me that he had gotten complaints from some of the players. They said that they did not want to play with me and wanted to play with the second string, upperclassmen libero, Eli (name changed for privacy and to not detract from the original intent of the book), instead. It was clear to me at this point that several of the upperclassmen were going into Coach Billy's office to try to get me off of the court.

My freshman year quickly devolved into an odd political proxy battle through the coach. It was a struggle filled with lies, confusion, and many losses for the team. The pattern would follow a general order. I would be told I was not starting for some very vague and untrue reason that was out of my control. If I did start, I would be pulled out after one error for a similarly strange and obscure reason. Per Coach Billy, the reasons for being benched were some of the following: I did not get along with the team, I did not look good in warm-ups, I looked nervous, I looked like I did not want to play, I looked sad, and made-up statistics that were unfounded by the post-game statistics report. Eli, or another libero, would start and perform at a level that ranged from passable to poor. If they started to underperform, I would then be thrown into the game. We would still lose. I would then be blamed for the loss due to poor passing or an insufficient number of digs. Repeat pattern. In some games, the pattern would break and I would be left in games at a time simply because I made extremely few errors or played perfectly. However, nothing could keep the pattern from inevitably repeating.

We finished the year with a 9-20 record. At my end-of-the-year meeting with Coach Billy, I told him everything. I described playing at Ship Weight was like trying to untangle myself from a jungle of vines. Before every game, I had to free myself from these distractions just to enjoy the sport. I had to fight the constant bullying from the upperclassmen, the constant worrying about being pulled from the match, the fear that I did not look happy enough to play, the fear that the upperclassmen were feeding lies to the coach, the feeling of being lonely in my hotel room because I felt ostracized from the team, and the feeling of being unsupported by my coach in the battle to improve the culture of the team. It was unbelievably exhausting. After sharing everything that bothered me about playing for Ship Weight University, Coach Billy looked confused. He told me that he had never kept me from starting or pulled me for the reasons that I stated. He completely denied not starting me because I did not get along with the team. He said that he started Eli the match after California because it took place in his hometown, completely contradicting our original conversation. I asked him about the other reasons for not starting me and he denied them all. He told me that the starting lineup was simply based on who did well in practice the week leading up to the game.

He lied to me in a one-on-one meeting. He then tried to deceive me into believing that I made up all of those reasons for not starting and being pulled during the games. How was I supposed to combat this? I told him that was not how I remembered it and he responded by vaguely answering and dodging all attempts to revisit the subject. He asked me if I had anything else to say before going home for the summer and I asked him about my athletic scholarship money.

This was the beginning of another battle, the battle for my scholarship. Upon recruiting me, Coach Billy promised that if I started, saw time on the court, and was a key player, I would receive some amount of scholarship money. When I asked about getting the scholarship that I earned, considering I played the most out of all the liberos on the team this season, he told me that my family was too "well-off" for me to receive any athletic scholarship. He lied to me again. Firstly, he knew nothing about my family's financial situation. Secondly, an athletic scholarship has nothing to do with the financial standing of the family; it is separate from financial aid. I knew if I challenged this, it would start an all-out war with my coach and I did not want to jeopardize my playtime. So, I let it go and told him I looked forward to next year.

MY SECOND YEAR

My second year started with the return of the four suspended players from the previous year, including Kevin, the older libero. Upon his return, it was clear that Coach Billy, based on the assembling of teams at practice, had given Kevin the starting spot back immediately. He did not have to re-earn his spot following his suspension. He did not have to demonstrate his commitment to the team nor did he have to confirm his ability as a player. I was incredibly angered by this. This was Kevin's *second time* being suspended at Ship Weight. I went to Coach Billy's office and expressed my annoyance that I lost my starting spot before we had even conducted three practices. Coach Billy assured me that no player had a solidified starting position.

Of the first seven matches, I started in one. The match I started in was an exhibition match with a DIII team that was very weak, so all of the non-starters played. Nothing I did in practice seemed to affect my probability of starting. No matter how well I played in practice, no matter how much I outperformed Kevin, and no matter how poorly Kevin performed in a game, nothing could get me into the starting spot that I craved so much. To my surprise, before the next match, Coach Billy called me into his office.

He told me I was going to play the next two matches.

My heart skipped a beat. I was so nervous. I was finally getting my chance to start and prove myself at the halfway point of our season. Then Coach Billy elaborated. He wanted me to go in as a serving substitute. I was to go in for one point each game of the match and serve a ball into the court and play defense. I felt humiliated and confused.

There was now no chance for me to be subbed into the game to play my original position. I wouldn't even wear the libero jersey.

Gameday arrived, and I had mixed emotions. On one hand, I was annoyed that I was out of the running for the libero position. On the other hand, I felt as if I should feel some amount of gratitude for being put into the game at all. During the first game of the match, I patiently waited to be subbed in but I was never called into the game. I figured Coach Billy had forgotten about me.

The second game of the match was nearing its end and Coach Billy, as promised, subbed me into the game to put a serve in and play defense.

I missed my serve.

I was not too bothered by my error, however. It was okay. Everyone misses a serve. I had more chances in the match and we ended up winning the game despite my miss.

The third game of the match approached its end and we had match point. Coach Billy subbed me in again and told me, "just put it in," as I entered the game. Everyone in the crowd cheered especially loud as I subbed into the game, almost as if they knew this was my one shot.

I missed my serve again.

The serve sailed way out past the end line. It was not even close. In men's volleyball, missed serves are very common for players who jump serve and are going for aces. That was not my case. I was simply trying to lob one into the court so I could play defense. That type of serve should not be missed, let alone missed twice. I was immediately subbed back out since I was promised only to play one point in the game. I jogged off the court attempting to hide my embarrassment and frustration.

When I reached the sideline, Coach Billy stopped me and asked me why I did not just put the serve in. I told him I was sorry and that I just missed it.

I felt like a complete failure. I felt like I was doing all of the right things but was not being rewarded. I worked hard at practice, I trained over the entire summer on my own, I felt I was outperforming Kevin for the starting spot, and I stayed out of trouble, but I was still not starting. Not only that, I was no longer even in contention for playing the position I was recruited for. I was now a serving sub who could not even serve the ball in bounds! I walked to the end of the bench choking back tears. Ship Weight scored the very next point to win the match and we lined up to shake hands with the opponent. After shaking hands with the opposing players, we shook hands with the referees. As I was desperately trying to get through the line and get away from everyone to hide the fact that I was not emotionally okay, one of the refs stopped me and said to me, "The crowd was cheering so loud for you, why couldn't you put that serve in for them?"

I lost it. I broke down crying in the middle of the gym, with everyone around, while my team was celebrating our win. I was completely devastated that my dream of playing Division I volleyball was not what I imagined it to be. A large portion of the team still despised me, I wasn't finding time on the court, and I was not having any fun. I stayed extra late in the locker room after the game and waited for everyone to leave. I then re-setup the net around 11 pm and served three buckets of balls over the net, unbelievably depressed.

About a month later, to my surprise, I got my first real start in match eleven of the season against the University of Charleston. Throughout the season, I had felt Kevin's performance was up and down at best, and our team was struggling enough for Coach Billy to make a change. I played excellently in the match and we won. For the next three matches, I was left in as a starter, unbothered. I remember playing close to perfection in this four-match stretch and we won all four matches. It was every non-starter's dream. I came off the bench and was given my chance. I absolutely crushed it and was rewarded with the starting spot. I was excited, happy, and relieved. I called my parents after the matches and told them how they went. From serving substitute back to my libero position, I was living my dream again.

After my fourth start in a row, we flew to California to play two more matches. Before our first match, we sat in a conference room outside of the gym going through our scouting report. When Coach Billy announced our starting lineup, I wasn't in it. I couldn't believe it. Why? I just played four flawless games in a row. What happened?

Kevin started and finished this match, and I was back to my spot on the sideline. I was furious and bitter. I remember hardly paying attention to the game and just lamented that I wasn't starting. I tried to figure out what I did to lose my starting spot. I replayed my performance in the previous week's practices in my head and compared it to Kevin's.

The next day, we played our second match. Coach Billy told me that I would start this match. I was incredibly confused as to why I was a starter again, but I did not want to question it. I was happy to be back in my starting position. I laced up for the match, warmed up with the team, and played with the starting six.

I did not make it through the first game of the match before being pulled. I was playing well overall but misread one tip from the opposing team. After pulling me out of the game, Coach Billy grabbed my arm and scolded me for missing the tip. He yelled manically about how it was embarrassing for me and the team for not reading this one attack. He then released me to the end of the bench. I was dejected but not surprised. I felt like the whole weekend was orchestrated. It felt like Coach Billy was searching for a reason to pull me from the game. I spent the entire first half of the season watching Kevin miss digs and make errors only to be left in. Now here I was, being pulled before I could even finish a set. It was the same pattern from my first year that I could not escape. I truly was on an incredibly short leash, and I hated it.

Upon returning from our California trip, I scheduled another meeting with Coach Billy. I wanted to get to the bottom of why I did not start the first match in California. According to Coach Billy, the reason Kevin started the first match was because he looked "locked in" during his extra reps practice the day before we flew out to California. I asked Coach Billy if I didn't look "locked in" during my extra rep practices. He told me I did but Kevin looked "really locked in."

My second year took a darker turn after this meeting. I felt completely hopeless. I could play flawlessly in practice and previous games, but still not start because of a gut feeling from my coach based on how "locked in" I looked. Every practice I tried to look more invested and play harder, but in the back of my mind I knew it would not affect whether I would start or not. In practice, I would get so angry when making an error because I knew if I did go in a game, I'd have to play perfectly and therefore errors were unacceptable. These circumstances drove me insane. I kept pushing so hard at practice only to find myself at the same spot on the sideline at the start of each match. I was so mentally broken that my performance spiraled. There was a point where I felt I was unable to pass a volleyball. I was getting worse and worse and angrier and angrier. I lamented going to practice because I felt like I couldn't perform well. To worsen the situation, I was still dealing with bullying from the upperclassman.

Toward the end of the season, I was subbed in one last time to play libero, but I was so mentally defeated that I played poorly and was immediately subbed out. I considered the whole year a wash, as I only played in four complete matches. I finished my second year with intense bitterness.

At the end of the year meeting with Coach Billy, I expressed my distaste. I told him I was extremely bitter about losing my starting spot because another player appeared extra "locked in" at one extra-rep practice. I complained to him that it felt like he spent more time trying to get Kevin back to a higher level of performance that he displayed before his suspension than developing me, the player that is not getting suspended, playing volleyball during the off-season, and doing everything right. He admitted that he was trying to get Kevin to his former glory and said he would try to be more objective in the future.

I asked for my promised scholarship again and he told me my family was too "well off." I left the meeting.

MY FINAL YEAR

I only spent three years at Ship Weight because I was fortunate enough to be able to accelerate my academics and achieve my degree early.

I returned to Ship Weight determined to end on a positive note and complete my collegiate volleyball career. I trained all summer again and re-commenced the battle to obtain my starting spot.

I concluded that Coach Billy had some sort of bias and favoritism toward Kevin and did not understand that I was the better libero. So, I made it my mission to prove that claim with statistics. Ship Weight used a statistics program called VolleyMetrics that recorded all statistics that occurred during a game. These statistics were incredibly detailed and I was fully prepared to spend hours proving my case and developing a report to present to Coach Billy to show that I was statistically out-performing Kevin.

When the first game arrived for our season and Kevin started, I could feel that this year was going to be the same as last year. It was going to be a year of me sitting on the sideline with intense helplessness. It was going to be another year of trying my heart out at practice, outperforming Kevin, and then watching all of my hard work be for nothing. I called a meeting with Coach Billy after our first game to convince him to change his mind about me.

In this meeting, I broke down every minute detail of our performances. I really focused on why I was not subbed in during certain games. I went through multiple years of statistics. I showed how I outperformed Kevin in many situations and would be subbed out. I showed how Kevin would be severely underperforming in other games and would be left in. I showed how I had better serve receive numbers, more digs, and more touches on the ball at certain points in the season. I remember this argument being very detailed, and we spent a long time in his office. He had many counterarguments for my report, but I had already planned rebuttals for his objections.

He countered by saying that since I did not get along with the upperclassmen, it made them uncomfortable when I was on the court. Therefore, they performed worse when playing with me. I then showed him proof that the other player's passing numbers are unaffected by which libero is playing. He then argued that since I do not get as many extra reps as Kevin does, I do not deserve to be on the court because I do not work as hard. I countered by informing him that I go in for extra reps once a week, which is the number he advised. He then argued that I appear panicky on the court after I make an error and that is why I am subbed out earlier than Kevin. I told him that performance should not be measured by subjective attributes, like how I appear, and should only be measured by the objective truth which is the statistics I presented.

It was at this point I could tell Coach Billy was starting to get furious. I had effectively proven that his decision for which libero would start was completely subjective and unfounded in the truth. I had proven that he treats me differently from Kevin and is more likely to pull me from a match earlier than Kevin. He took a minute after his last argument and seriously looked at the statistics. He looked through every statistic and found one that Kevin outperformed me in. The statistic was "digs that lead to kills." He told me that this statistic was the most important and that since I did not have better numbers in this category, I simply could not start. I was flabbergasted by this argument. The statistic he chose was so obscure and unimportant that I didn't even know what to say. After a libero digs a ball, it is up to his teammates to set and score the point. The libero has no effect on if his dig leads to a kill. This statistic is borderline arbitrary in its own right. Still, I tried to rebut. I argued that since I got more touches and more digs in general, it is likely I will have a lower percentage of digs that lead to kills. However, it is still better to get more digs that don't lead to kills and keep the rally alive than to simply not get the dig and lose the point.

He rejected my argument and stuck to that statistic no matter what. I told him he was clearly looking at the statistics to bolster his biased decision to start Kevin as opposed to using the statistics to figure out who to start. After I said this he leaned forward, got real close to me, and yelled at me, "IF YOU'RE SO UNHAPPY THEN WHY DON'T YOU FUCKING QUIT!" I was bewildered. I thought this was what he wanted. He always encouraged the team to come into his office to talk about starting time, volleyball, or anything that bothered us. I managed to muster a reply. I said I did not want to quit and that I just wanted to play. I made an excuse to leave and got out of there as fast as I could.

My bewilderment by his comment quickly turned to resentment and even faster to contemplation. Maybe he was right. I was constantly angry, annoyed, frustrated, upset, and overall unhappy. A few more games with me sitting on the bench went by and the thought of giving up and quitting took over my consciousness. I sat on the sideline of these games completely miserable with intense anguish. I was tired of feeling this horrible, so I called Coach Billy the following Monday and asked for another meeting with him. He said he was available on Thursday. That Thursday was going to be my last day as a collegiate volleyball player. I was ready to quit and an unfamiliar wave of peace radiated through my body. But with this peaceful feeling came sorrow and a sense of defeat. I prepared myself to live with this defeat.

However, my plan was quickly thwarted when Kevin and a few other seniors got in trouble one night and were suspended for eight games.

I was now the starting libero again. Just like that.

I was terrified.

I felt guilty for feeling this way. I should have been ecstatic. I finally got the one thing that can alleviate my mental anguish. The one thing I had been fighting for. The main reason for my meeting to quit had been instantly resolved in one night, and all I could feel was terror. Mentally and emotionally, how could I go from the peace of quitting to being thrust back into the belly of the beast? Thrust back into the game of trying to prove myself and prove that I deserved to start from the beginning?

I had to decide. It was Thursday, I had my meeting scheduled, and our team had a game that Saturday.

I canceled the meeting. That Thursday night I sat down with my-self and brainstormed how I could get myself emotionally and mentally ready to play. I had to overcome all of these feelings so I could perform, and I needed an answer fast. What I needed was a philosophy to believe in; a philosophy that could purify my mind and allow me to play the game that I loved.

The philosophy I came up with is one I still enact to this day. When I play pick-up games with my friends, in my professional league, and even video games on my couch, this philosophy has taken me very far. I am excited to share the idea I hold so precious to my heart.

CHAPTER 3

Shedding More Light On The Representation Of My Origin Story

Before I share my philosophy, allow me to clarify a few things. It is easy to demonstrate my time with Ship Weight Volleyball as an incredibly negative battle where I was the victim of cruel teammates and a biased, angry coach. It is easy to present myself as a successful underdog whose love for the game propelled him to the top where he belonged.

But the truth is that my time at Ship Weight is far more complex; too complex to write in a standalone book.

To speak about the school itself, I adored Ship Weight. The academic side of Ship Weight treated me well, and I have many people to thank for offering me such an excellent time. It was strictly the volleyball part of my college experience that was jaded.

Elaborating on the complexity of the volleyball experience becomes odd. Some of the people who jumped me my freshman year I would consider my friends today. There were some upperclassmen teammates who were nothing but nice to me. Even the upperclassmen who bullied me showed times of mercy and compassion. As for Kevin, I really liked him. Despite contending for the same position, he was a thoughtful guy and once even advised Coach Billy to start me if I was playing well.

Some days I loved volleyball. Some days I hated volleyball. My coach was sometimes nice to me and other times was awful. Some days Coach Billy made my life difficult. Some days I made Coach Billy's life difficult. Some days I felt I could do no wrong in my position. Other days, I could not pass a single ball to the target. Some days I played better than Kevin, and other days he played better than me.

But I strongly believe that this complexity better encapsulates the typical trek of a student-athlete. Maybe being jumped by your teammates and screamed at to "fucking quit" is unrelatable, but the other multileveled experiences most certainly are relatable. The complex experiences of having trouble getting along with teammates, dealing with teammates that are inconsistent emotionally, feeling like you have to prove yourself when given a chance to play, sometimes hating your sport, dealing with emotional anguish, or dealing with a coach you feel doesn't like you. These are the problems that are incredibly likely to be faced and alter student-athletes. I believe the overall emotional turmoil that comes with the complexity of each individual's journey is shared among most student-athletes. And, I believe if I were given proper advice on how to face just a few of these common challenges, I would have been much better off.

If I could do my time at Ship Weight again with the knowledge I have now, I would do it much differently. A lot of my mentalities, decisions, and interactions with my coach and team were wrong and that will become increasingly clear throughout this book. Hopefully, I can help you avoid those same pitfalls.

CHAPTER 4

How To Think Of Yourself As An Athlete

What philosophy did I come up with to cure myself of the demons swimming in my head preventing me from enjoying my time in the sport? I call it Ryan Alu's Robot Philosophy, or RARP for short.

I decided to treat my mind like a computer and my body as a tool my computer was controlling. I was a robot with no emotions. I was simply a machine, trained at performing specific volleyball tasks. Just like how a computer performs tasks without question or emotion, I performed my volleyball tasks without question or emotion.

To better elaborate on my philosophy, I must break the explanation into two categories: the logic behind RARP and what RARP did for me.

THE LOGIC BEHIND RARP PART 1 (MATH)

In my time of need, I took what I understood well and turned it into a philosophy. At Ship Weight University, I majored in computer science and math. I really enjoyed statistics, especially applied statistics. I thought it was fascinating that statistics could be applied to real-life scenarios such as sports. I was so interested in statistics that in the summer between my first and second year at Ship Weight, I became a mentor for a week-long math camp. The camp, held by the Ship Weight Math Department, taught 15 high school students about statistics in sports in exchange for college credit. My responsibility was to sit in on these classes during the day and entertain the kids at night.

By sitting in on these classes, I learned just how impactful math was in the world of sports. I learned about William Benter, the man who made nearly one billion dollars on horse betting by developing a better machine learning algorithm that considered more variables to produce more accurate odds of a horse's success. I watched Moneyball, the 2011 film about the 2002 Oakland A's baseball team that was assembled purely based on statistics, disregarding conventional baseball etiquette and knowledge. I learned that statistically speaking, hockey goalies should be pulled earlier when losing a game, and football teams shouldn't punt the ball away as much on fourth down. I learned that slumps and hot streaks are not real and are simply a misunderstanding of random sequences.

All of these scenarios treated the respective sport like a simulation. There were no emotions, no feelings, no good days, no bad days, no hot streaks, no cold streaks, and no superstitions. There were just numbers, odds, statistics, math, and truth. It was pure. So why was I not thinking of myself like that?

When I go to the casino to gamble, I know the odds of winning are not in my favor. When I lose money, I don't think it is due to having a bad day, not wearing my lucky jacket, or because I didn't get enough sleep. No. I am just another pawn in the ever-vast chess board of gamblers. I am just a statistic. The odds are not in my favor, and I lose unsurprisingly.

When I go to the horse track and bet on the horse that has its odds listed at 65-1, I know this horse is very unlikely to win. If the horse wins, I am ecstatic because I win a lot of money. But my only thought is that I am simply fortunate that the horse won even though the probability of the horse winning was so low. I never for a second think the horse won because it had a good mindset, or because I had a good mindset, or because the horse tried extra hard, or because the horse was extra focused, or because the horse had a good night's sleep, or because the horse wasn't nervous, or because the horse felt extra confident. No. I just treated the horse like a statistic.

Why am I treating the horse like a statistic and not myself? Why am I treating myself like a statistic when I gamble and not when I play volleyball? How can I understand the logic behind the movie, Moneyball, but not apply that same logic to myself when I play?

THE LOGIC BEHIND RARP PART 2 (SPEEDRUNS)

During my senior year of high school and first two years of college, I performed speedruns of one of my favorite video games, Super Smash Bros. for the Nintendo 64. Speedruns are instances of completing a video game as fast as possible. From 2017 to 2019 I held the world record for completing the story mode with Mario in the fastest time. I learned quite a lot from achieving this record, and inspiration was drawn from this experience when hashing out my RARP philosophy for volleyball.

In order to set the world record with Mario, 14 stages had to be beaten with near-perfect execution. To complete a stage, I had to defeat non-playable computer characters (CPUs) by knocking them off the edge of the stage. These 14 stages can be broken down into two categories: The CPU makes the correct moves (completely random) and I make the correct moves. Not only did I have to perform all of the correct combos and button presses perfectly, the game had to arbitrarily move the CPUs the correct way allowing for the optimal run. For all of this to occur in one run was unfathomably unlikely. It was so unlikely that it took me thousands of tries for everything to line up perfectly, not to mention the countless hours of inventing and practicing the correct combos and movements.

To give you a better idea of what was needed to make the perfect run, I used to break down the 14 stages in terms of the probability of successful execution. The probability for "in my control" was how consistently I could perform the action. The probability for "out of my control" was how likely the game randomly made the CPUs move the correct way.

STAGE 1: Mario vs Link

In my control: Throw, FAIR attack, z-cancel, throw, b-down spike.

Probability: 90%

Out of my control: None. Link moves the same way every time.

Probability: 100%

STAGE 2: Mario vs Yoshi Team

In my control: Chase Yoshis in the correct order with correct movement.

Probability: 85%

Out of my control: Two Yoshis do not land on the opposite platform and perform a quick jump animation.

Probability: 70%

STAGE 3: Mario vs Fox McCloud

In my control: Throw, dash attack, throw, drag down.

Probability: 80%

Out of my control: Fox initially walks the correct way. Fox does not perfectly tech-role my dash attack.

Probability: 40%

STAGE 4: Break the Targets!

In my control: Run off the edge.

Probability: 99%

Out of my control: None.

Probability: 100%

STAGE 5: Mario vs Mario Bros.

In my control: Perfectly time a throw where Mario hits Luigi out of the air. Tornado spike.

Probability: 50%

Out of my control: Mario initially walks right.

Probability: 50%

STAGE 6: Mario vs Pikachu

In my control: FAIR attack. Tornado spike or grab the ledge.

Probability: 90%

Out of my control: None.

Probability: 100%

STAGE 7: Mario vs Giant Donkey Kong

In my control: Down air, down smash, grab twice, up smash.

Probability: 80%

Out of my control: Donkey Kong does not jump. Teammate CPUs do not put too much damage on Donkey Kong.

Probability: 60%

STAGE 8: Board the Platform!

In my control: Jump off the edge.

Probability: 95%

Out of my control: None.

Probability: 100%

STAGE 9: Mario vs Kirby Team

In my control: Tornado attack or grab Kirbys.

Probability: 90%

Out of my control: Kirbys do not spawn on opposite sides of the stage at the same time.

Probability: 50%

STAGE 10: Mario vs Samus Aran

In my control: Throw, up smash, up air, up smash, up air, up smash.

Probability: 70%

Out of my control: Samus does not move to start.

Probability: 50%

STAGE 11: Mario vs Metal Mario

In my control: Grab spam to the ledge. Down smash.

Probability: 90%

Out of my control: Metal Mario does not jump back on the initial ledge.

Probability: 30%

STAGE 12: Race to the Finish
>> In my control: Get to the end of the maze.
>> Probability: 95%
>> Out of my control: None.
>> Probability: 100%

STAGE 13: Mario vs Fighting Polygon Team
>> In my control: Tornado attack enemies.
>> Probability: 90%
>> Out of my control: Enemies land on favorable platforms together.
>> Probability: 20%

STAGE 14: Mario vs Master Hand
>> In my control: Alternate combos for maximum damage.
>> Probability: 95%
>> Out of my control: Master Hand performs a majority of favorable attacks (zero or one missile gun attack).
>> Probability: 50%

To the readers that do not play any version of Smash Bros, this is a bunch of jargon. Nonetheless, please allow yourself to focus on the probabilities as that is the main focus of what I am trying to convey. I can calculate the probability of getting the world record by multiplying all of the stage probabilities together. The probability of obtaining the world record by having a perfect run where the game does everything right and I do everything right was .006%. That is about 1 out of 16,666 tries.

When I was going for this record, I understood that the "1 out of 16,666 tries" was a reasonable estimate for success. Maybe it was 5000 more or 5000 less but I knew that I would likely have to try thousands of times before I obtained the record.

What this understanding did to me emotionally is hard to describe. The understanding of the probability of success and the understanding of my probability of successfully completing an individual stage, changed how I thought about myself. I became completely removed from everything. I became removed from the end result, my performance, and myself. I no longer thought of myself as me. I thought of myself as a detachable object dropped off at a simulation to perform. My body and my hands, sitting on my couch, were no longer a part of me. Instead, my physical being was a robot that I had trained to perform this specific task. I let the robot do its thing.

It was as if you asked a person to flip a coin and have it land on heads eight times in a row. The probability of that occurring is 1 in 256, but if that person sat there long enough and flipped that coin, eventually it would happen. It might not happen in a day or a week or a month but it would happen eventually. This is how I felt with Super Smash Bros.

Early on, in my first hundred runs before the separation of my mind and body fully set in, I remember having a run where the first 13 stages were perfect but I made an error on the final stage resulting in missing the record by only a few seconds. I was enraged. My initial thought was that I was so close. But as time went on and hundreds of more runs passed, I learned that I was not close. The truth is that it did not matter where the error occurred. An error could happen in the first stage or the last stage, it did not matter because the end result was a failure. This is the truth of math. A run where nothing goes right and a run where everything goes right except the final stage is exactly the same. They are both failures and equally "close" chances of success. Each attempt at the world record after this realization had no feeling. Failing meant nothing. Making an error meant nothing. I was just a machine of probability pulling on the slot machine lever of fate.

Soon I found that my quest for the world record gave me a feeling of purity. There was something beautiful and relieving about the understanding that I was not in control of my performance. My performance and I were two separate entities. There was me, and then there was my physical being, my body, and my hands, in the simulation.

I realized, relating the idea back to collegiate athletic performance, I was completely and utterly not in control of how I performed. I was simply a robot with a certain percent probability of success. If I made six errors in a row in a speedrun, I did not think that there was something wrong with me, or that I sucked at video games, or that I was having an "off" day (whatever that even means), or that I should quit, or, maybe most importantly, that the errors I previously made had any impact on the probability of making future errors.

If I made six errors in a row, I understood that the probability of that occurring is low but still possible and I was completely unphased. It is the same for trying to flip a coin to get heads six times in a row but instead getting tails six times in a row. Should I be devastated? Should I think the coin is broken? Should I think the coin is having a bad day? Should I think the coin needs a break? No. Of course not. If I understood all of the logic behind speedruns and knew that my performance on a specific run has nothing to do with me and all to do with the probability of success resulting from practice, why am I not applying this logic to myself when I play volleyball?

THE LOGIC BEHIND RARP PART 3 (ESPORTS)

In my second and final years at Ship Weight, I played on the collegiate esports team where I mained Yoshi and King K Rool in Super Smash Bros Ultimate for the Nintendo Switch. On the team, we would practice by playing against each other and opponents online. For matches, we played in a league and had games every Wednesday. Outside of school, I also played in local cash tournaments.

I greatly enjoyed my time with esports and have a special sense of pride that I was able to be a part of a competitive video game team. However, that dreaded game, Super Smash Bros Ultimate, was a terrible, evil game. From projectile spamming Villagers, to relentless back airing Marios, to untouchable speedy Sonics, to asinine Game and Watches, to sword characters that could neutral air me from a different zip code, to Pikachu's 45-minute combos, to Luigi's 0-to-death grab combos, to the game's infinitely many unfair, annoying, and gimmicky combos that any player could learn and master in a very short time, this game was broken.

Admittedly, after hundreds of hours of practice and playing, I was fairly good. I did well with my characters (they were lower-tiered but I grew fond of them), I was the leading player on the school's team and used to finish respectfully in my local tournaments (9th in tournaments with upwards of 64 contestants). Performing well brought me great joy but losing unlocked a level of rage and anger inside of me that I did not know I was capable of. I admit, with great shame, that during my stint as a collegiate video game athlete, several controllers were launched and destroyed in fits of rage that made the devil himself look like your friendly local ice cream truck driver.

My anger was so out of control that I accidentally broke a $3,000 television in my school's computer science lounge where I practiced on my own. I threw my water bottle after losing in the final seconds of a match, it hit the corner of a footrest, bounced, and flew straight into the bottom left corner of the flat-screen tv. It was at this point that I scheduled several meetings with Ship Weight's school psychologist to help me with my fits of rage. Although this story brings me tons of shame, it is vital to understand just how angry I could get while competing in this game.

The psychologist helped me find ways to avoid my intense anger when losing. She identified (and was correct) that most of my anger originated from the discrepancy between reality and my expectations. The problem was that I falsely expected to win every game, and when reality did not match my expectation I was left with a feeling of "I SHOULD have won that game," which caused my insurmountable anger. Controlling expectations in a match is vital advice, but it was the next lesson I learned that truly affected my RARP philosophy.

Now that I was able to avoid getting irreversibly angry during a match that was not going my way, I noticed I was playing significantly better. Even more noticeable was my ability to make a comeback after going down early in the match. Now, many will stop here when analyzing themselves, but I really wanted to get to the bottom of why I was performing better. Sure, I could say being angry doesn't help you win in a match, so don't be angry. But *why* was the anger making me perform worse in my video game matches?

I determined that while I was angry, I was not critically thinking. In the Smash Bros world, this is called autopiloting. When a player is autopiloting, he will approach the enemy the same way over and over and over because this approach is the most comfortable for the player. The player will go for the same combo, the same setups, the same smash attack, the same dodge-roll direction, and the same way of getting up from the ledge, repeatedly. In other words, the player will not learn from the intricacies of the match and will perform the same actions again and again regardless of the result. Autopilot cost me a lot of games. I would start out winning, my opponent, who was critically thinking and not autopiloting, would learn my patterns, and then I would make no adjustments and lose.

I needed to avoid autopiloting at all costs. To do this, I controlled my expectations and emotions. I tried to have as little emotion about the game as possible because I knew anger (or sadness, bitterness, nervousness, or even too much adrenaline) could force me into autopilot. The other thing I did was remind myself to critically think. In between sets, I took more time to think about the game. What is my opponent doing? What moves worked at the beginning of the set that no longer work? Which way does my opponent move after I throw him? Even in between lives in the middle of the set, I would stay on the respawn platform and use all of my respawn invincibility time to THINK. How can I outsmart my opponent? What is he doing? What am I doing? How can I win?

If I could positively impact my performance by critically thinking and controlling my emotions for Super Smash Bros, why wasn't I doing that for volleyball?

THE RESULT OF RARP

After developing my philosophy and vowing to stick with it like my life depended on it, I transformed myself into a robot and stepped back.

I, as a volleyball athlete, was an extension of myself that I placed on the court and allowed it to perform. I, Ryan Alu, was a different being than the volleyball athlete robot. The robot's performance was outside of my control. I saw myself as a statistic that others could gamble on and I saw volleyball matches as a simulation for my robot self to perform practiced actions. I never once worried about if the robot got enough sleep, if it was mentally ready, if it was rusty, if it was having a bad day, if it was focused, if it was in its own head, if it was nervous, if it was properly prepared, or if it had any other emotional, cliche, mental worry or fear that every athlete has. Just like how I never think of the horse on the track in this fashion, I stopped thinking of myself in this fashion.

I saw myself, my robot self, as a simple conglomeration of odds. If a ball was served to my left I had an X% chance of passing a perfect pass. If it was served to my right, a Y% chance. Passing float serves had *this* percent chance of success while receiving jump serves had *that* percent chance of success. If I did not like those odds during the match, it did not matter. Those were the odds. If I wanted those odds to improve in my favor, I would improve at practice after the match. The same logic with my speedruns applied to volleyball.

Even though I sent out my robot to play volleyball, that robot was not an autopiloting fool. Throughout the entire match, I critically thought, so that the robot could learn midmatch and not get stuck making the same error over and over again. When the robot made an error, I, the brain of the robot, would swoop in and tweak it. Together we were a learning bot. We were artificial intelligence.

Let's say I was just aced short to my right. I used to get nervous, angry, sad, annoyed, and emotional. I used to get disappointed in myself. I used to lament that I SHOULD have gotten that serve. I would look at the bench to see if I was going to be subbed out. I would get consumed by the dread that I was blowing my chance as a starter. I would then make no adjustment because I was too worried about feeling and thinking all of that nonsense.

Instead, I asked new questions. Is this the server's favorite serve? Did he serve there last time? How can I increase my chances of success? Did I perform a familiar bad habit that leads to lower chances of success? Can my teammates help me? Then I make a decision. I am going to move my robot body one step closer to the server so I don't get beat short again. I have now avoided autopiloting, adapted, and slightly increased my chance for success. I was a robot but a critically thinking robot.

RARP was very freeing. RARP cleared my mind. RARP was my savior.

CHAPTER 5

Finishing My Collegiate Volleyball Backstory (With The Power Of RARP By My Side)

It was the day of my first game as the new starter, days after I made peace with quitting and almost followed through with it. I was unbelievably nervous. The same determinantal thoughts rushed through my head. This was my final chance to prove to myself that I was the rightful starter all along. Maybe I should have quit. Maybe I'm not good enough. What if I get pulled? What if I don't play well?

Everything had to be in perfect order too. I had to wear the right socks. I had to have my jersey tucked in the exact right amount. I had to make sure I slept at least eight hours the previous night. I had to wear the right underwear. I had to drink extra water throughout the day. I was superstitious.

I slowed myself down and thought about RARP. I sat in my room for a long time before the match and applied RARP to overcome each fear and thought. My self-talk and thought process went as follows.

"I am nervous." Why? I have trained my body to perform these actions my entire life. I cannot control how my body performs, it just

comes down to the odds of success. Am I nervous when I bet at a casino? No. There's no sense in being nervous, Ryan. We do not have to be nervous because there is nothing in my control to be nervous about.

"I hope I don't play poorly." There is no sense in hoping. There is only the truth. Playing well overall is too broad to think about anyway. A robot only thinks about individual actions, one at a time. I have prepared my body and I accept the odds of success for every volleyball action. It is time to run the simulation and hope has no effect on the simulation. Stop hoping for an outcome, Ryan. It doesn't make sense to hope, there is just the event occurring.

"I have to prove to myself that I deserved to start all along." Robots don't prove anything. They just do the action. I have no control over what is proven anyway. The statistic of "if I've proven myself" is not measurable. These thoughts are useless, Ryan. It is just taking space away from critically thinking about what the opposing team is doing and how I can adapt.

"I hope I don't get pulled." I cannot control whether or not I get pulled. Robots do not fear or think about something outside of the game itself. Again, this thought is a waste of brain space for critical thought.

"I have to wear the right underwear and socks and be perfectly comfortable and ready." Does wearing the right underwear and socks affect my probabilities of success? No, they don't. I never think about my socks or underwear ever during the game anyway. Even if they did somehow impact my performance, it would be so minuscule that my odds of success would change by virtually zero. It doesn't matter how the robot is dressed or if it "feels comfortable." The robot just does the actions it practices. Robots don't feel. I don't need to feel comfortable because it statistically does not matter.

"I have to drink extra water." Water is important, but will it affect my odds of success? No. My position requires far more technique than it does stamina. My odds will be unaffected if I am a little thirsty. Hell, even if I were dehydrated with a headache, the training I went through

in the past made the volleyball moves I do *automatic,* so a headache would not affect my actions.

I continued this logic for every non-RARP belief until I was left with nothing. I had no thoughts about the game. The game simply was. It was an event in the future. It was equivalent to a meeting, a class, a party, or an appointment. I do not think about events when they are in the future. They are on the calendar and I go to them when the time comes. After applying RARP, the game was just another fun event in the day. It lost all of its negative connotations.

There I was dressed for the game, wearing my school colors, representing the program that had thrust me into a crazy mess of highs and lows. I felt like an adventurer in a jungle. In front of me was the task at hand, the sport I loved, the way out of the jungle into freedom. Behind me lurked animated vines that relentlessly wrapped and grabbed my limbs, dragging me backward. These vines were the bullying remarks from my teammates that disliked me, the snide remarks about my ability from my coach, the self-induced detrimental thoughts throughout my time at Ship Weight, the lies behind my lack of scholarship, and the superstitions I held onto about my play.

I turned on RARP mode, blew those vines away, walked to my freedom, and played excellently that match. For the first time in my entire collegiate experience, I was able to fully enjoy my sport. There was no more sadness, bitterness, fear, or anxiety. I felt loose, carefree, and was having *fun.* With RARP, the same joy I had when playing volleyball for my high school, my old club, and with my dad in the front yard came rushing back to me. I felt the purity again that volleyball gave me in the past. I was free.

RARP truly was my saving grace and the more I focused on applying RARP the more confident I became as a volleyball player and a person. I noticed that since I spent less time focusing on things I could not control, I found it easier to accept and become unphased by difficult and unfortunate situations. This freed my mind to simply do what I believed was right as opposed to being overwhelmed or crippled by the fear of potential consequences.

Previously, I did not want to confront Coach Billy on his lies about my scholarship money for fear that it would lead to less playtime. However, with my newfound confidence in RARP, I did not care about the result that I could not control. I knew that Coach Billy lying to me about my scholarship was wrong and I knew the right thing to do was to stand up for myself and confront him.

I scheduled a meeting with Coach Billy and told him that I wanted the scholarship money that he promised me during my recruitment. I found court time in all three years and was a main starter for two. According to his promise, this was more than enough to receive some kind of scholarship. Coach Billy informed me that he would speak to the athletic director and see what she could do for me. The next day he pulled me aside after practice and told me that he spoke with the athletic director. According to Coach Billy, she said there was nothing Ship Weight could do because my family was "too well off."

So, I went straight to the athletic director and asked her if Coach Billy had spoken to her about my scholarship money in the past day.

She said no.

The next day arrived and Coach Billy pulled me into his office, visibly angry. He scolded me for going behind his back to the higher-ups to get him in trouble. I told him that I did not try to get him in trouble but was simply trying to discover the truth about why I could not get an athletic scholarship. He then proceeded to yell at me that I was not getting a scholarship because there was no money left in the scholarship pool. I asked him if Kevin received any scholarship money. He told me no. Later, I found that was also a lie, revealed by Kevin himself. I thanked him, shook his hand, and left.

This meeting would have normally been very difficult for me. Before RARP I would have been emotionally devastated by the anger Coach Billy showed me. But this time I was unaffected. I did not receive any money, but at least I secured some sense of honor in myself. I implemented RARP, stopped fearing something I could not control, overcame a difficult situation, and just sought out the truth and what was right.

After that meeting, Coach Billy's behavior toward me changed dramatically. It was evident, at least to me, that he wanted to see me fail. He would make up stories and once told me after a game that he talked to the opposing team's coach about me. He lied and said that the coach said I was the worst passer on the court. When asked by the freshmen about the time I was jumped, he retold the story and informed them that I deserved it. During a different match, when I made an error, he yelled to the backup freshman libero to get ready. He directed his voice toward the court, to me, in an attempt to make me nervous about being pulled from the game. He would scold me for being late no matter how early I arrived on the bus for away games. It seemed like his goal was to try to break my spirit.

As the season progressed, the relationship between my coach and me became uglier and uglier. This meant I had to mentally overcome more and more vines to be able to play well on the court and enjoy the sport I loved. But it did not matter how many vines there were. RARP would always eliminate them all. No matter what negative dig Coach Billy would throw my way, it would have no impact on my performance. My robot body would hear the information, disregard it because it had no impact on my probabilities of success, and continue on its way. I was emotionally and mentally invincible and my performance reflected that. I was playing unbelievably well and it seemed like there was nothing that could stop me from doing so.

Before the season could progress any further, the NCAA canceled it due to the COVID-19 outbreak. Even though that was the conclusion of my collegiate volleyball career, RARP lived on.

Upon graduation, I was recruited for the Tennessee Tyrants in the National Volleyball Association (NVA) in 2020. In this league, I implemented RARP to quickly adapt to the new environment, a new type of ball, a new coach, a new level of play, and a new team. At the end of the championship tournament, I was awarded the all-tournament team best libero award. Not only did RARP help me prove I was a top passer in the league but it allowed me to have fun, which in itself is beautiful. I continued to play in the NVA playing for the Chicago Untouchables (2021) and The New Jersey Freedom (2022) where I was selected to participate in the all-league all-star match.

In the NVA, having undergone nearly two years of personal RARP training, I noticed how peaceful volleyball became. Everything was very pure. I stopped being nervous before matches. I stopped thinking only about my own performance on the court. I stopped thinking about how I appeared on the court. I stopped worrying about making errors. I stopped trying to prove myself. I stopped worrying about what my teammates thought of me. I stopped worrying about my preparation before games. I stopped worrying about whether someone I knew back home would watch me underperform. I stopped being embarrassed when making an error. I was able to focus on the game and how I could help the team win. I simply walked onto the court, played volleyball, and had fun.

RARP has continued to help me in my personal life too, freeing me from nagging negative self-talk, confidence issues, and overall social discomfort. The freedom RARP provides me is nearly indescribable and I will cherish the philosophy forever.

After having two years to reflect on my experience at Ship Weight, I realized that there were a lot more circumstances where I could have applied RARP. Allow me to share with you my advice.

CHAPTER 6

How To View Yourself As A Teammate

There are infinitely many cliche books and articles about the basics of how to be a good teammate. If you are playing a collegiate sport, you have most likely been a member of a team for the majority of your life and know that you must sacrifice for your teammates. You have already understood and internalized information like, "there is no 'I' in team," "sacrifice yourself for your teammates in order to win," "treat people the way you want to be treated," and other obvious teammate etiquettes that the majority of athletes follow.

Everyone thinks he is a great teammate. I would gamble that if I were to go to any collegiate team and casually ask all of the players individually if each of them is a good teammate, they would all say yes. The only problem is that you are probably not a good teammate. And it's not because you're not sacrificing enough, or you're not caring enough for your teammates, or because you didn't give a freshman a ride from the dining hall, or because you didn't help a teammate with their homework, or whatever nonsensical, over the top, exaggerated commitment coaches push for. You're probably a bad teammate because you do not understand what you signed up for when accepting the offer to play at your college. This is not your fault as it would have to be explained to you by your coach, who probably didn't explain this to you. But still, this lesson is incredibly valuable and the earlier you learn it, the better off you are.

YOU'RE A PAWN

When you accepted an offer from your school, walked on, or whatever, you signed up, via obligation of signature (or maybe even financial compensation in the form of a scholarship) to be a member of a system and do a specific job at the discretion of your coach. This means you are a pawn on the chessboard. You're not a knight, you're not a bishop, you're definitely not the rook or the queen, and you are absolutely not the king. This means you are an employee at the biggest corporation full of managers, managers of managers, bosses, and panels of bosses at an infinite scale. This means you are a cog in the most complex clock. This means you are a soldier enlisted in the ever-scaling military system. This means you are not important and you certainly are not important enough to have any managerial duties or ideas.

Take this real event as a perfect example for better understanding. When I was a freshman at Ship Weight University, I scheduled and held a meeting with my coach because I had a great idea to help our team win more games. I wanted to be a good teammate, and I believed that my idea would increase our probability of winning. I wanted to show Coach Billy I was an engaged member of the team and really cared about how the team performed. My idea was to practice more deception with the setters and practice less with the speed of the set. Up until this point, Coach Billy only focused on the speed of the set. He wanted to get the ball to the pin hitter as fast as possible to ensure a late (and thus weak) block. I argued that the speed was too fast, the hitter and setter were not connecting, and the same late block could be ensured if the setter was more deceptive and faked the blockers out.

He disagreed with my idea, said our setters were not good enough to be deceptive, and sent me on my way.

What I did seemed harmless, but in reality, it was incredibly stupid and conceited. I was a pawn that tried to be the king. I was a warehouse employee that tried to tell the CEO how to run his company. I was a cog that removed myself from my position to tell the other cogs how to turn. I was a soldier that marched into the commander's office and offered military strategy. It was conceited of me to think that my idea was right. It was conceited of me to think that my idea should be heard. Most importantly, it was conceited of me to promote myself and take on managerial duties when I accepted a contract to be a player and not a coach.

You might still think otherwise. "But Ryan, you were just trying to help your team win. Surely that is good intent, right?" I did have good intentions. But the effect will have the opposite of what is desired. Try to think of what happens when too many players promote themselves and give themselves managerial duties.

I know for a fact that I was not the only player going to Coach Billy's office and offering strategies on how to win more games. Multiple players were trying to take on managerial duties. The probability of all of our ideas being the same was basically zero. So now, we are all trying to do our jobs while pushing the team in different directions. Maybe I say to my setter, "hey try to trick the middle blocker this play" (I didn't, but a player who believes he has managerial duties easily can), while another player begs the setter to set slower (against the coach's desire for a fast set), while another defender plays defense in a different spot than what the coach ordered because he believes he is more effective in his preferred spot. All of this creates chaos and prevents the team from being in unison with the coach's vision. It also distracts every player from getting better at their given role.

What does all of this mean? This means that your coach is the King, the CEO, the largest cog, and the president. This means that you are not important and you must follow whatever your coach says no matter how foolish or wrong you might think he is. If he tells you to play a different position, play a different style that you're uncomfortable with, sit the bench, come out of the game after making only one error, serve the ball under the net, play hard through the most uneventful and boring practice, do nothing at practice, do everything at practice, or be completely and utterly ignored, you must do it. You must do it because it's his team and not yours.

Even if you know that what your coach is saying is completely wrong and counterintuitive to winning, you must do it because you did not sign up to help your team win. You signed up to be a member of a system in order to create a winning *organization*. This means it is not about your four years at the school. It is not about you *at all*. You might be a four-year experiment run by your coach that fails. If that is the case, you helped your coach and your school eliminate a strategy, therefore, furthering the development to find the winning strategy.

This is a very difficult lesson to learn. It seems almost counter-intuitive. In order to help your team more, you must admit you are not important, stay in your own lane, and focus on your own job. This is probably much different than what you are used to. I know it was incredibly different for me. On my club team and in high school I was one of the best players and my coach encouraged me to lead the team. I was a leader, had managerial duties, and other players looked to me for advice. I was a part of a family. This is not the environment you signed up for. You are a part of a system now. If you think you and your school are the exceptions, you are dead wrong.

THE PERFECT EXTENSION OF RARP

This idea of being a pawn is an extension of RARP. Once again we see the same strategy of differentiating yourself from you. You are a robot sent in to do a specific job and increase your position's odds of success. If everyone is a robot doing their own task, led by one com-mander, your coach, your team's chance of success increases. And if it doesn't, your coach will tweak his strategy to increase success like how you tweak your strategy to increase your position's success.

This is very intimidating. Sure, thinking of yourself as a robot may not be that hard because your brain is still the commander of your body robot. But now, you have to consciously give control of yourself, your robot version of you, the one that does the actions, to someone else.

I had trouble with this. Whenever Coach Billy would teach me a new skill to practice, I would always approach each instruction with great suspicion. I am a very analytical person and I treat all new information as false until I prove it true. This proves valuable in most situations. Collegiate athletics is unfortunately not one of those situations. This is not RARP. A robot does not question instructions from the programmer and your coach is a higher-up programmer than you. His instruction is more important than yours. Your coach likely knows more about your sport than you do. If you think you are the exception, you are wrong.

I understood that I should have listened to the coach without question but I still struggled immensely with doing so because of one very common fear. I feared that if I learned something new and practiced it, I would mess up older, successful habits. For example, let's say a coach told me that my arm swing needed changes a, b, and c. I feared that if I implemented a, b, and c and I got worse, I would not remember my old arm swing and ultimately have no arm swing, resulting in me performing worse than my original situation. If you have this fear it is okay because it is irrational and can be easily dispelled from your mind.

I believe the brain is a very capable tool for controlling your body. It is never bad to learn new techniques because your brain will optimize your body. Instead of forgetting skills, your brain will naturally incorporate the new with the old. So, instead of learning a, b, and c and then completely overwriting your working skill, your brain will create some new, perfectly optimized, combination of the old and the new. Your skill may drop slightly at first because you are trying something new, but you have to make sacrifices in order to grow. You have to take that initial hit in order to gain skill and reach new potential.

"But Ryan, what if my coach does not know what he is doing and is teaching me bad habits?" The probability that your coach is teaching you negative skills that will make you worse is very low. But even if that is the case, oh well. When you perform worse with your newly learned negative skills you allow the coach to see the effect of the taught skill. Your coach will learn from this and adjust his coaching. Remember, you signed up to your school as a sacrifice to better the program over multiple years, not to become a better player. It is bigger than just you, you have no control, and you agreed to this. If you really are in this position where your coach is teaching you negative habits (you probably are not but think you are), play during the off-season and learn different strategies and techniques either through self-experimentation or with a different coach.

Mentally becoming a pawn is super beneficial. If you haven't noticed yet, becoming a pawn and RARP fall under the same category of thought. We are challenging what we really are in control of. It turns out we can control very little. The more problems we find in the we-can-control-category that actually belong in the we-can't-control-category and put them there, the more brain space we create to focus on the things we can control. You stop becoming frustrated by trying to control things you can't and thus feel better mentally.

By extending RARP and becoming a pawn, you can avoid the all too annoying and frustrating meetings with your coach on why you're not starting, bickering about the direction of your team, the fear of implementing new ideas, managerial duties of questioning instruction or leading the team, attempts to befriend or maintain a relationship with your coach, attempts to better the team, mentally taxing thoughts of "if only my team did this," and other problems out of your control.

This is how you should see yourself as a teammate. You are a pawn, you do your job, and then you go home. It is up to your coach to push the team in the right direction and it is completely out of your control. You signed up to be a member of a system that does his exact job. You did not sign up to get better as a player, be a starter, extend your athletic ability, or *whatever reason that involves you.* It is NOT about you. It is NOT about you. It is NOT about you. If you do not understand that this is what you signed up for, you need to change that now.

HOLDING YOUR TEAMMATES ACCOUNTABLE

Many coaches will tell you that you need to hold your teammates accountable. Coaches will tell you if your teammate shows up late to practice you must tell him that his tardiness is unacceptable in order to hold him accountable and ensure you are being a good teammate. If your teammate skips a rep to get done earlier, you are to tell him not to do that so you can hold him accountable and ensure you are being a good teammate. At the same time, all of your teammates are expected to do the same to you when you fumble or are slacking.

This is completely stupid. Do not hold your teammates accountable. If your coach tells you to hold your teammates accountable simply do not obey. Period.

"But Ryan! You just said to be a pawn and follow your coach's orders no matter what." This is true. You must be a pawn and follow your coach's orders no matter what since this is what you signed up for. However, sometimes a coach will instruct you to perform a logic contradiction. A logic contradiction is a state where two things are simultaneously existing that cannot. Imagine if I ordered you to breathe and hold your breath at the same time. This is impossible, one cannot both hold their breath and breathe at the same time. It is impossible as they are exact opposites. If a coach instructs you to perform a logic contradiction, you cannot perform the instruction. You cannot follow his command not because you are being disobedient and refusing to be a pawn, but because you literally cannot.

The instruction to hold your teammates accountable is a logic contradiction. One cannot be on a team and hold a teammate accountable, it is not logically possible. The definition of a team is a group of EQUAL individuals unified to accomplish a common goal. It's a group of equal pawns. All of the pawns are equal in level of power. So how can you be a pawn and a bishop at the same time? You cannot. A pawn cannot tell another pawn where to move. A co-worker cannot command another co-worker to come to work earlier. A soldier cannot command another soldier to do more push-ups.

It is not your responsibility. You are a pawn and a player, not a coach or a manager. "But wait, Ryan! My position requires me to tell people what to do!" This is different than self-promotion and holding your teammate accountable. A goalie tells defenders who to mark. Liberos tell hitters where to stand in serve receive. Hitters tell setters what is wrong with the set. This is different because it is implicit in the contract that you signed when committing to your school. These instructions are a requirement of the position. To be a goalie, you must tell the defenders who to mark. This is an implicit responsibility of the goalie. To be a defender, you must listen to your goalie when marking players. This is an implicit responsibility of a defender. However, across all sports, no position has an explicit responsibility to perform team managerial duties. No position has an implicit instruction to reprimand your teammate for showing up late, skipping reps, faking sickness, faking injury, lying, not lifting enough weight, or not getting enough extra reps. If you reprimand your teammates for doing these things you are not a teammate holding other teammates accountable, you're a pompous jerk that has decided that you can be a coach when you feel like it.

The intentions of the hold-your-teammates-accountable philosophy are pure. The thought is that by pushing each other to achieve more you can move toward victory with greater ease. In actuality, it does the opposite. All this philosophy does is make you hate your teammates and your teammates hate you. Many will argue that holding your teammates accountable would work if only players were not so soft and could take criticism. This is simply not true. It is a natural and correct reaction to be annoyed or angered that an equal feels compelled to suddenly become a superior; when a player suddenly feels compelled to be a coach. It is completely natural to dislike someone who is conceited and thinks that he can promote himself without justification and tell you what to do. Holding your teammates accountable is fundamentally flawed and there is no saving or defending it. Focus on perfecting your own position. Focus on your own timeliness and your own commitment to completing all reps of a set. Focus on yourself. Do not hold your teammates accountable. It is not your responsibility, leave that to your coach. If he does not hold your teammates accountable, oh well.

It is not your responsibility.

CHAPTER 7

How To Deal With Your Coach

Your coach probably sucks at his job.

Most coaches, especially in the typical collegiate athletic program, have not been trained to be coaches or good managers. Some coaches have not even played the sport that they are coaching! However, you most likely have coaches that were good players and found themselves in coaching positions at the end of their careers.

A good coach can be rated by two criteria: knowledge of the sport and managerial skill. Out of ten, your coach is probably a 9/10 for knowledge of the sport and like a 3/10 for managerial skill. Before I explain how to deal with your coach, allow me to explain what your coach should be like and what a good coach looks like.

THE PROBLEMS WITH COACHES

Just like how you should think of yourself as a pawn or an employee at a mega-corporation, your coach should think of himself as the boss. His job is to lead the team in a militant fashion, leaving no room for ambiguity.

One major problem with coaches is that they are too lethargic and slow. A good coach runs a very clear practice, with a focus on efficiency like everyone is always slightly running out of time. The coach starts practice with a clear warmup that does not drag on 30 minutes into the practice. He starts a drill, explains its purpose extremely quickly, and then runs it. Too often coaches explain drills for far too long expanding into the tens of minutes of talking. Coaches shouldn't say so many words as it bleeds into the time of getting reps. The drill starts quickly and is tweaked as players push the drill's rules to the limit. There should be no time for players to dilly-dally about and not be doing anything. There should be no drills where players are waiting in a line, just standing there.

Another major problem is that many coaches run drills that are uncreative, brainless, and pointless. The majority of drills should not be super basic, boring, or require little skill. Drills should be complex, fast-paced, game-like, and purposeful with multiple players focusing on different aspects of the game. I used to be subjected to a drill where the players would roll the ball over the net (a basic drill that 98% of players can already perform) for 40 minutes. Most of the time we succeeded but sometimes we failed simply because we were so bored, unchallenged, and disconnected from the purpose of the drill (if it even had one) that we would inevitably forget to care. Then the bad coach yelled at us for not being able to complete the drill justifying its need for the drill (DAMN!). Drills should be intense and imaginative. Everyone should be challenged, learning new valuable skills, and trying to be successful/ win in the drill at the same time. Who cares if the drill breaks down and is ugly, at least the players are critically thinking.

I understand, that some vital drills cannot be saved from being repetitive and boring (like training footwork). However, these drills should be the exception, not the rule, and they should be offset by a clearly defined purpose with fast-paced urgency to maximize reps.

Many coaches are non-RARPers, which is incredibly tragic for you. They get angry and yell at you, they pick favorites based on their feelings, they interpret statistics incorrectly because they are not intelligent or good at math, they are superstitious and make game-time decisions based on their superstitions, and (worst of all) they think that they have way more control over the game than they actually do. A good coach understands that when the game starts, the probability of success is fixed, and there's no amount of screaming or substitutions that can really change that probability.

Finally, the absolute worst mistake your coach is probably making is relinquishing managerial duties to his players. This one is absolutely satanic. A coach should NEVER give you managerial duties. My coach should have NEVER encouraged me to try to change the culture of the team. That was his job and he failed to do it. It was not my responsibility and he threw me to the wolves to let me die in emotional anguish as I tried to change the team's culture through his encouragement. Giving pawns managerial duties is cruel. Players in college do not have the life experience nor the power to enforce any command in order to have managerial duties. Here are some real examples of coaches that I know that have given managerial duties to players.

One coach brought the freshmen into a meeting and had them pick words that will define their team for the next four years. *What*? I am 23 years old and I can't even pick a word that will define me for the next day! How is a naive 18-year-old, who is just becoming accustomed to a new school and a new sense of freedom going to shape the goal and outlook of an ENTIRE TEAM? An 18-year-old does not even know who he is as a person. He is not going to know which words will best define a team. The freshman is just going to pick arbitrary words like honor, accountability, and honesty and go home thinking he did something. It's the coach's job to set the goals that define the team. It's HIS team. If you don't think this is insane, take a synonymous scenario. Let's say you are a new hire as an accountant at a multimillion-dollar technology company. Now, the CEO comes to you directly and asks you to define the goal of his company. It's ludicrous. What do you know about running a company, you were hired to crunch numbers. I can't see how the logic would be any different for a company that generates wins (your college team) instead of generating software (the technology company).

Another coach I knew instructed the players to pick teams for a 6v6 scrimmage. Already, this is a bad start because it's the coach's job to pick teams and do managerial work. The players lagged and stalled not wanting to discriminate among their own teammates. They felt uncomfortable picking one player over another to be on their team. This was a reasonable complaint as it should not have been the player's job to determine who were the best players. The players stalled and would not pick teams for so long that the coach called everyone in for a meeting. He then asked all of the players as a group of about 20 to share why they felt uncomfortable in a democracy-type style where everyone had to share. This quickly devolved into a time-wasting debate. Some players felt fine picking teams. Other players felt uncomfortable picking teams. Some players complained that they were wasting time. It devolved into chaos because democracy absolutely sucks. Don't believe me? Let's see what our founding fathers had to say about democracy.

John Adams: "Democracy, will soon degenerate into an anarchy, such an anarchy that every man will do what is right in his own eyes, and no man's life or property or reputation or liberty will be secure and every one of these will soon mold itself into a system of subordination of all the moral virtues, and intellectual abilities, all the powers of wealth, beauty, wit, and science, to the wanton pleasures, the capricious will, and the execrable cruelty of one or a very few" (An Essay on Man's Lust for Power, August 29, 1763).

George Washington: "It is one of the evils of democratical governments, that the people, not always seeing and frequently misled, must often feel before they can act right; but then evil of this nature seldom fail to work their own cure" (Letter to Marquis de LaFayette, May 10, 1786).

James Madison: "Democracies have ever been spectacles of turbulence and contention; have ever been found incompatible with personal security or the rights of property; and have in general been as short in their lives as they have been violent in their deaths" (Federalist 10, November 22, 1787).

This is why the U.S. is a democratic *republic*. It's because democracy is chaos. Everyone can't get their way on the team. It is up to the representative, your coach, to lead the team and take charge.

Another example is when a coach I knew ran a player-led practice. This is always a disaster because half of the team will want the practice to be intense and the other half of the team will want the practice to be relaxed and a big joke. This inevitably causes frustration among the team as individual players try to step up and take control of the practice. This causes contention because no player has the right or power to self-promote and run the practice. Imagine if your coworker tried to hold a meeting to inform everyone that they are not trying hard enough. It is absurd and everyone will hate this coworker. It is the same thing when a player tries to run a practice. It is cruel for a coach to put a player in this situation.

In all, if your coach does anything previously mentioned, he sucks. If he runs a 30-minute warm-up, has uninspired drills, is a non-RARPer, is emotional (too angry, too sad, quick temper, etc), or gives you or your teammates managerial duties, he sucks at coaching. If you feel like you have a job other than being a player (practicing, playing, lifting, watching film, eating right, etc) your coach sucks. If you feel like you have additional power and can control what the team does at practice or who starts, your coach sucks at his job. If your coach asks you for advice on how to run the team, your coach really sucks.

So your coach probably sucks, what should you do about it?

DISTANCING YOURSELF FROM YOUR COACH

In the past, you have probably been encouraged to have a good relationship with your coach. If you are not starting, you were probably advised to work extra hard and show the coach how much you care. If you show your coach that you are really trying and putting in the extra work he will reward you. I'm sure you have been advised, even by your own coach, to pop into the office every once in a while and talk about school and your sport. Many recommend becoming almost buddy-buddy with your coach and updating him on your life. I've been advised before to tell my coach when I am extra stressed and emotionally troubled and to use my coach as a mentor.

All of this is completely stupid. Do not do this.

Distance yourself from your coach and let him do his job. Again, you are an employee at a mega-corporation and your coach is the boss. As an employee, you are not going to be friends with the boss. You each have your own roles to perform for the betterment of the system.

Do not try to schedule meetings to create facetime and develop a relationship. If your coach offers you a ride back to your dorm, decline it. If your coach asks how school is going, be as general as possible. When practice ends don't hang around to talk to the coach, just leave. Don't schedule meetings to see what you can improve upon because if your coach hasn't already told you, he doesn't know or have an answer for you. Don't show your emotional status to your coach. If you are having a bad day, hide it at practice and talk about it later to a friend or counselor. Do not go into your coach's office to strategize about the game or improve your team. Do not text your coach during the off-season. Just show up, do your job, and go home.

Your coach is not your mentor, guidance counselor, therapist, or friend. He is your coach. He is there to win games and create a winning program. He is there to use your skill as a player the way he pleases and it has nothing to do with you as a person.

This may seem like a contradiction to my previous statement of always listening to your coach and doing what he says because you are a pawn. But if your coach is trying to self-promote to another role that is outside of coaching, like being your friend or mentor, then he is falling into a logic fallacy and ordering you to do things that cannot be accomplished (like breathe and don't breathe). So, if your coach orders you to have a meeting with him about something other than your sport, you should decline it and say you are only comfortable discussing the elements of the game and your responsibilities as an athlete. If you are less brave, go to the meeting but be as brief as possible and keep it short. If he asks about your family just say everything is good and don't reveal any information. If he asks about your mental state or emotions just say that you are good and get out of there. Remember, this only applies when your coach is trying to transcend the realm of being a coach. If he holds a meeting with you to tell you that you need to get your physical in to be eligible to play or that you need to come in for extra reps to practice a specific set, you better be all ears.

It is better this way. Again, we are narrowing down the things that you can control. The responsibilities of a player do not include establishing a good relationship with the coach. Establishing a good relationship puts a responsibility on you. If you have this responsibility, you feel the need to invest time in the relationship. It especially gets dangerous when you begin to believe that the effort put into this relationship will lead to something you want, like more playtime. Establishing a close relationship with your coach does not provide you with any perks and is a waste of time. It is a waste of precious mind space that can go toward bettering yourself, bettering your skill, and enjoying the game more. Stay out of the politics of relationships and go enjoy the game.

As a last note, you may fear that not establishing a close relationship will cause your coach to dislike you and lead to less playtime. You may fear that if you are too aloof, the coach will forget about you. This is not true. If the coach holds this reason against you to justify your lack of playtime, he is lying. He is simply looking for a reasonable excuse to not play you and justify his arbitrary decision-making process. If it isn't aloofness it will be something else that is completely subjective like how my coach did with me. Protect your mental state, distance yourself from your coach, and apply RARP. It won't have any negative side effects like jeopardizing playtime.

HOW TO DEAL WITH MANIPULATIVE AND NEGATIVE FEEDBACK FROM YOUR COACH

A valuable life lesson is to break down assumptions of power. An assumption of power is to believe by default that a person in a position of power is something more than just some guy living life with what he's got. Sometimes we get caught up in believing that our superiors are perfect, non-human, beings. This lesson is usually learned when your professor in elementary school is wrong and teaches something objectively not true. When this happens, the assumption of power is broken and the truth is revealed that your professor is just some dude.

Your coach is just some dude. He's just a person. Maybe he doesn't really care about his job. Maybe he doesn't really care about you. Maybe he feels unfulfilled and just goes through the motions for a paycheck. Maybe he loves his job. Maybe he is super insecure. Maybe he is very superstitious and illogical. Maybe he's a super angry person who hates his life. Who knows? So, if your coach comes at you with intense negativity, blind rage, insults, and yells of insanity, do not become emotional.

The worst thing you can do is fall back into the assumptions of power. Do not let yourself believe that since you are being yelled at by a superior, you are a failed player and have done something incredibly wrong. Do not let yourself become devastated or scared. The interaction is no deeper than some dude yelling at you over a game that completely does not matter in the scheme of life.

You must implement RARP. You cannot control that you are being yelled at, intensely confronted, or given manipulative feedback. Crying or becoming angry will only hurt you. Lock down and step outside of yourself. Let this dude scream at your robot body as you step back and watch. While you are chilling and taking in the absurdity of a grown man yelling at you and trying to manipulate you over a game invented for fun, try to pick out any valuable information.

Pulling valuable information out of a terrible delivery is incredibly difficult but unbelievably valuable. It is not enough to activate RARP and completely disassociate. You have to try to figure out what your coach wants and see if there is value in his words so you can grow as a player.

Let me give you an example. My coach at Ship Weight once pulled me aside and told me "You are not playing as good as you think you are. On defense, it looks like you are playing dodgeball and are afraid of the ball."

Cool.

When I was told this my initial reaction was total consuming rage. I was overwhelmed at how multidimensionally wrong the statement was. First, according to the stats in my freshman year, I was leading the conference in digs until I was pulled toward the end of the season. Second, I am not afraid of the ball. Third, this doesn't add any value to my improvement. Fourth, even if I did think I was playing better than I was, why would a coach try to make his own player less confident?

What is the correct RARP answer to this? The best response would have been:

"Okay, how can I improve my defense?"

This ignores the negative aspect of the comment, proves the comment is ineffective at disrupting your emotions (because you are a robot), and attempts to find out if there is any value in the coach's comment.

Did I say this at the time? No. I was not practiced enough at RARPing to tackle this level of challenge. Would I say this today after practicing RARP for multiple years? Yes. If you can implement RARP and respond to manipulative and negative feedback by being emotionless and authentically trying to find value in the statement, not only are you an elite collegiate athlete, you are an elite human on Earth, capable of doing a lot in this world.

UNDERSTANDING YOUR COACH'S PRIORITIES

College coaches and high school/club coaches have different priorities.

Up until this point, it is likely you have only experienced family-oriented team environments. In a family-oriented team environment, your coach acts as a parental figure and your teammates act as siblings. The relationship you have with the coach resembles a teacher-student style where your coach is the mentor and you are the mentee. In this environment the coach's priorities are ranked as follows:

1. Your personal growth in life
2. Winning games
3. Financial gain

Financial gain is ranked third because many high school coaches earn very little. Some club coaches are volunteers and are not paid at all. Many of these coaches work for the satisfaction of making a difference in younger people's lives as opposed to trying to make coaching a career.

Winning games is ranked second because many high school and club coaches care about winning but it is not the end all be all. These coaches are more likely compared to college coaches to sub players into games that are less talented to ensure everyone gets a chance to play and grow as a person.

The ultimate goal is your personal growth in life. High school and club coaches will do things like stop practice to teach life lessons, try to help you learn valuable skills like honor and integrity, and try to help you understand your emotions and be a part of a team.

The family-oriented team environment makes perfect sense when the priorities are in this order. Back in high school, your personal growth in life was ranked at the top because you were a KID! You were not an adult yet!

You are no longer a child. You are an adult now and you are treated as one. In college, that means your team's environment is no longer one that is family-oriented. It is corporate-oriented. In a corporate environment, the coach is the boss and you are the employee. The coach's priorities are ranked as follows:

1. Financial gain
2. Creating a winning legacy
3. Your personal growth in life

Financial gain is ranked first because, for college coaches, the team is their full-time job. They are not going to coach the team unless they are being paid.

Creating a winning legacy is ranked second because many coaches want to do well in their job. No coach wants a losing record and if they keep losing they'll be fired. So they have to create a winning program and legacy or they are out of a job.

Finally, there's your personal growth, at the bottom. And third is a generous estimate. There could be ten other priorities before your personal growth. It could be argued that your personal growth is not a priority at all but simply a courtesy that the coach has because he's a nice person.

It is imperative for you to understand that you are no longer in a family-oriented environment and your coach's priorities are different. As stated before, it is not about you anymore. Understanding this will help you control the expectations you have for your coach and help prevent you from getting emotionally blindsided by your coach's actions.

DEALING WITH CAPTAINSHIP

Let's say your coach makes you the captain. What should you do? The answer is to reject your captainship. Do not become a captain.

Becoming a captain may seem like a great honor and a very rewarding experience. The idea behind creating a captain for the team is to have players be able to find leadership in someone more relatable than the coach. It is a fellow player that others can rely on when the game is close or the team's morale is low. This is just another idea that has good intentions but ultimately fails in practice. The result of captainship is the sowing of distrust and resentment among teammates.

The idea of captainship on a team finds itself in the logical contradiction category. One player cannot have more power than other players on a team because a condition of a team is that all players are equal. When a player becomes a captain they are cruelly put into a position of power without any way of enforcing said power. It's like putting a child in a lion's den and telling him he is a lion tamer. Can a captain punish other players for misbehavior? Can a captain make players run sprints? Can a captain kick players out of practice? Can a captain pull someone from the match? The answer is almost always no. So what is a captain other than a puppet?

Most of the time, coaches, in an unbelievably selfish manner, will pawn off administrative responsibilities to the captain. The coach will treat the captain as a liaison between the coaches and the team. He will task the captain with responsibilities of enforcing player-led practices, ensuring everyone shows up to their extra rep session, enforcing the 48-hour rule of no alcohol, or making sure everyone understands the standards of the team. How in the world is the captain supposed to do this with no real power? He can't.

When the captain tries to do what his coach orders of him and tries to complete his managerial duties, he will be met with great animosity from his peers. Any human's initial reaction to an equal trying to tell him what to do will always be negative. The teammates will immediately presume that the power of captainship has gone to the captain's head, that he is taking his captainship too seriously, and that he is being annoying, pompous, and uptight. One result is the captain becoming frustrated that he and his team are underperforming because he cannot complete his impossible tasks. The other result is the captain's teammates growing tired of the captain, instilling an underlying hatred in the team culture.

If you are not the captain and you want to be a captain, you are wrong. If you are currently the captain, try to do as little as possible with the title. If you find yourself in a position where you are the non-captain and your captain teammate is trying to tell you what to do, please have patience. You are watching the cruelty of a coach ordering a pawn to do an impossible task. Help your captain and feel sorry for him because it is not his fault. He is probably under a lot of stress and needs your assistance, even if you think he has become too arrogant and bossy.

CHAPTER 8

How To Deal With Not Starting

When you are younger, not starting is easier. Usually, there is a chance to simply leave the team and join another one. In my case for volleyball, if I did not start, I could always go to a neighboring club or play for my own club's B team. There always seemed to be more options if you wanted to play and "start." But at the collegiate level, it is different. You are stuck physically, since there is only one team at the school, and stuck emotionally, since you want to carry out this dream you had to play at your specific school or at your specific level.

Now you're in a tough position. You have committed all of this energy and time to your sport, thought you were traveling to a new place to excel at this craft (not what you actually signed up for), and achieved the dream of becoming a collegiate athlete, but you don't get to play in the games. At Ship Weight, this killed me. It's heart-wrenching and it is not an easy situation to deal with.

When it comes to playtime, the most common thing a coach will do is put the responsibility of starting on you as the athlete. When I went into Coach Billy's office and asked him why I wasn't starting, I was always given an answer containing the same theme: I was not starting because of something *I* was doing. I didn't get along with the team, I didn't get enough digs that lead to kills, I needed to practice my defense,

I wasn't getting enough extra reps, or I needed to be in the gym more. It was always my fault and in my control.

After your coach puts the responsibility of not starting on you, he will probably say something like this, "You need to push yourself to try to catch the starter and take his spot. This will put pressure on the starter to try harder, thus pushing him to get better. If everyone on the team feels the pressure of someone trying to catch them, then we are uplifting the level of play because everyone has a reason to play hard." This is completely stupid and just makes all of your teammates hate each other.

I believe the idea that you are responsible for your starting time and the idea that you need to catch the starters are complete fallacies. It is probably the worst thing a coach could say to his player and these ideas are setting you up to fail.

Not only that, but since players have been fed this lie over and over, their teammates will probably give them the same advice in an even less tactful way. Let's say you are struggling with not playing, you do not know how to handle this new situation because this is most likely one of the first times you have not been a starter. You go to your teammates for support and your teammates feed you the same garbage your coach just did. "Stop whining! If you want to start you have to put more effort in. Get extra reps. Yada yada yada." Now you have the entire team telling you that it's your fault that you don't start. It's incredibly tragic and false.

Let's be very real and blunt. The truth is that your starting time is basically completely out of your control. Over the years, in many different sports, I have been advised by coaches to try three different routes in order to increase my starting time. These routes will probably sound familiar to you. You can befriend your coach, you can do extra chores and go above and beyond, or you can train extra hard. None of these routes work the way you think they do.

STRATEGY 1: BEFRIENDING YOUR COACH

In the case you do not start, many will encourage you to interact with your coach more. Make more meetings with him, get noticed by him, and become his friend. This does not work at all.

Whether you deserve to start or not, the sad truth is that there is nothing you can say to your coach that will change his mind. You will never have a meeting with your coach and walk out of that meeting suddenly a starter. You could do what I did and go the scientific way with statistics. I statistically proved that I had better numbers across all skills in my position at certain points in the season but it did not change anything. You could have the most passionate argument, you could have the most logical argument, and you could have a message from an oracle. No conversation will promote you from a bench player to a starter. Most coaches do not even care about statistics, and even if they do, most do not have the mathematical ability to correctly interpret them. Most coaches make decisions based on a gut feeling or an initial interpretation of you that can be completely unfounded. So no form of talking, debating, or communicating with your coach will result in you suddenly starting when you are not.

You can do something else a little further than communicating; you can manipulate your coach. This is a very low route. A few players at Ship Weight went this route. They would strategically set up multiple meetings with the coach in order to get facetime. In these meetings, they kissed up to the coach. They talked about everything but volleyball and tried to make the coach feel good about them. I always thought this was one of the saddest things a student-athlete could do. They completely stripped themselves of any dignity that they had in order to get onto the court.

This manipulation strategy had tragic results. Most times it changed nothing. But sometimes it led to a single start. But, it did not matter. During this single start, the player was held on the shortest leash imaginable. If the player made a single error he would be taken out immediately. The coach is not giving you a chance to succeed. Usually, he is giving you a chance to prove his original theory correct that you do not deserve to start. It is a self-fulfilling prophecy. So, the manipulation technique should really be ruled out. Are you really going to destroy your dignity and tarnish your character just to be given one game where you will most likely be yanked after the first set, leaving you with an even darker feeling of missing your chance?

In short, befriending your coach will not help you start. Setting up meetings and showing you are "engaged" does not work either. Nothing you can say to your coach will work. Manipulation doesn't really work either. Whether you start or not is out of your control.

STRATEGY 2: GOING ABOVE AND BEYOND

Another technique is to go above and beyond, outside of the scope of your sport. The idea here is that maybe you are close to starting and just need a little edge to get that starting spot. If you are a really good student, are involved in the community, and are an upstanding teammate, your coach will reward you with a starting spot. This is not true.

You can ask your coach what you can improve on, be the first one in the gym and the last one out, have excellent grades, lift more weights, turn on 110% effort, clean up leftover trash in the gym, be the most encouraging teammate, and do 1000 hours of community service. Guess what, this won't help you. It is like trying to get a raise at your job at McDonald's by joining the National Honors Society. Your manager at McDonald's does not care at all about your extracurricular activities. He only cares if you do your job at McDonald's.

Your coach does not care about what you do outside of your sport. He might say he does, but he does not. Maybe he cares about having a good attitude (if you're lucky because that is in your control) but he probably doesn't.

Nothing you do outside of the realm of your sport will affect your starting time. Whether you start or not is out of your control.

STRATEGY 3: TRAINING EXTRA HARD

Let's now analyze the final reason. Certainly, you might think, if you practice harder and get more reps you will start.

Maybe.

Let's say that you do not deserve to start and are actually the weaker player. You are less skilled than your teammates that play your position. This is where your coaches and players tell you that you need to try harder and get more reps. But this does not work the way you want it to. At the collegiate level, all players are getting exceedingly closer to their peak performance marker. Imagine a graph like the one below.

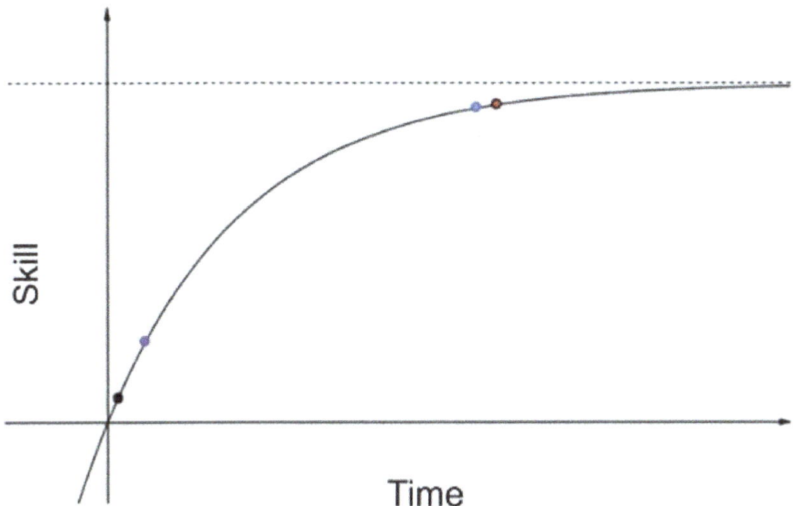

Let's say that the horizontal asymptote is the best you as a player can ever get. In college, you're approaching this asymptote. Obviously, you are not at the asymptote as there is plenty of room to still grow. I think I am a better player now than I was at Ship Weight and I'm sure other professional players don't think they were better in college after playing 10 seasons overseas at higher divisions. But still, the closer you are to this asymptote, the more hours it takes to move closer to your peak performance. The time it takes to get from the blue dot to the red dot might take 4 to 5 seasons of playing volleyball every day for 3 hours a day. Meanwhile, the black dot to the purple dot might take 5 hours.

If you don't like graphs, let me tell a story. When I first played the video game Super Smash Bros Ultimate, I was at my friend's house. When we both started out playing the game and unlocking characters for the first time, we were both pretty even in skill. He would win some games and I would win some games. I then spent the second half of the semester (6 weeks) training at the game to join my school's esports team. I played for 2 hours every day, 5 days a week. That is 60 hours of training. My friend only played casually and logged another 20 hours. When I came back and played against my friend I absolutely destroyed him. There was no contest. The difference was day and night. There was only a difference of 40 hours of practice time between us. When you begin training a new skill, you can fly along this curve.

Now take this story. Our best hitter at Ship Weight, James (name changed for privacy and to not detract from the original intent of the book), unfortunately, became ill and was out for the entire off-season. The NCAA limits all collegiate off-season time (or at least for volley-ball) to eight hours a week during the off-season. For Ship Weight, we divided that 8 hours in the following way: 3 hours were spent lifting and 5 hours were spent playing volleyball. Our semester lasted 15 weeks. That is 75 hours of missed volleyball for James. Every other hitter got the opportunity to have a 75-hour leg up on him. When James came back the next season, he was still the best hitter. It was like nothing happened. Those 75 hours made no discernable difference between James and every other hitter on the team. By the time you are at college, it takes A LOT of hours to creep along the curve.

Let's say you are the blue dot and the person who has the starting spot is the red dot. Contrary to what your coach insists, you are not a few extra reps away from overpassing that person. That gap might be 700 hours of repetitions. Let's be generous and say the gap is 400 hours. There are about 75 weekdays in a semester at Ship Weight. Let's assume you go in for extra reps every day for 1 hour. Extra reps are in addition to the normal number of hours you are already playing during practice. 400 needed hours/75 days = 5.33 semesters. That is a little more than two and a half school years.

Wait, there is more. It is not even enough to just catch the red dot. You have to seriously overtake the red dot because if you match skill level, the original starter will probably still play out of the coach's habit. So, you now have even further to go along the curve to get the precious start time. That means even more hours of practice time.

Not only that, this is under the assumption that those extra reps you get are quality reps. Most of the time these reps cannot be guided by the coach or he will be in violation of going over the allotted coaching hours per the NCAA. In most sports, you can't even get extra reps by yourself. In basketball, at least you can go set up the rebounding machine and shoot by yourself for hours. How do you practice volleyball by yourself? You can't just pass the ball to yourself or against a wall. This practice is good for beginners, but the practice you need at this point is in-game scenarios: hard hits, hard digs, and hard serves. Now, you are forced to practice with other players. What if the starter you want to overtake is interested in getting extra reps with you?! All of the previous math was under the assumption that you are getting extra reps *over* the person you want to overtake. If the starter is getting extra reps then you have to do even more hours or else the distance between you two will remain fixed! You move along the curve together.

You can't just get extra reps and try harder to get your starting spot. Your coach is lying to you. Your teammates are lying to you. With the trying harder and getting more reps technique, you might overtake the starter sometime in more than 5 years. Are you in school that long?

Jeez, this is really negative stuff. Is it possible to overtake someone in skill at this level? Of course. The real time to make up these hours is whenever the team is not together. For volleyball, our school had the entire summer off. Over the summer, I would log nearly 30 hours a week playing volleyball. I was in three leagues that held games once a week and would play in all-day tournaments every Saturday and

Sunday. For those counting along, that is 30 x 15 = 450 hours over the summer. And these 450 hours of volleyball were in competitive, high-level settings. Every weekend, prizes that ranged upwards to $2000 were in contention, so you can imagine the competition was strong, solidifying the quality of my rep time. I logged 450 hours playing high-quality volleyball. Although I have no proof, I do not believe Kevin logged nearly as many hours and I still wasn't the coach's pick.

Now did I play 450 hours of volleyball because I was hatching out a grand scheme to start in the second half of my collegiate career? Of course not. I simply loved volleyball. I still log nearly 450 hours of volleyball every summer and I am two years out of my undergraduate career. This is incredibly rare. I suspect most collegiate athletes hardly play their sport in their off-season. When obtaining my graduate degree at Dartmouth, I spent a lot of time with the women's varsity volleyball team. At Dartmouth, there is a six-week break from Thanksgiving to New Year's. When all the girls came back from this break the coach asked them via a show of hands if they played any volleyball over the break. Not a single player raised their hand. Not one player played over the break. A similar situation would occur at Ship Weight where players would return from summer break and be absolutely terrible for the first few weeks of practice, clearly showing they hadn't played in months. There's nothing wrong with not playing, but it really puts everything into perspective.

Let's be real. No one wants to start so badly that they are going to reroute multiple summer breaks. If you are not logging 450 hours in your sport over summer break, you probably are not going to all of a sudden change and want to do this. The truth is, your drive for spending this much time in the off-season with your sport cannot come from the desire to start in season. It has to be at the core of your being. The love for your sport has to be so strong that you want to play it ALL of the time.

THE RECAP

So, what does all of this mean to you? Let's recap. You want to start. For whatever reason, you are not starting. You realistically have two options to find the court *MAYBE*. You can get your five seconds of start time at the expense of your dignity and character by logging in hours kissing up to the coach that you probably resent for not starting you. This will lead to you getting pulled from the first or second game you start, leaving you with the "I blew my chance" feeling, which is a very dark place. Or, you can rework your entire summer break and commit it to playing your sport as often as you can at a high level. Let's be real, if this is not already happening, it's not going to happen (maybe it will but it's incredibly unlikely). Neither of these techniques even guarantees start time because, in the end, you can be the better player and still not start.

If you're not going to dedicate your summer break to playing your sport, how can you get rid of this horrible feeling that comes with not starting? You cannot let this feeling eat you alive. It is a scary place to be in when this feeling manifests. It starts with feeling upset. Maybe you call your parents a couple of times in tears because you are working so hard and now you feel unrewarded. Then it leads to you standing on the sidelines, faking wanting to be there even though you are dying inside. Suddenly you start rooting against the starters. You hope they fail so you can get subbed in. You hope they sustain a season-lasting injury so you can get your playtime. You start hating the starters. People who were your friends are now your enemies because they play and you don't. You can't hang out with them outside the sport because your hatred is just too strong. Maybe you start saying mean things to them. Maybe you bad mouth them to the coach. It's a twisted and evil place and I've seen it happen to players.

Is this the type of person you want to be? When your sibling and parents show up to the game do you want them to know how you are thinking about your own team? Is this how you want to represent yourself in this world? People are looking up to you. Maybe you have a little brother that looks up to you. Maybe he is amazed that you are a collegiate athlete. Maybe a younger player from your club used to watch you play and wishes he were you. Maybe he models his play around you. Maybe he watches videos of you playing. And now, here you are, sitting on the bench, swarming with demons. Do you want that younger player to look up to this version of you? Whether you start or not, you are an excellent player. You are further along that line on that graph than the majority of all players in the world. In college, you get to develop your character and control what type of person you become. You want to develop yourself into your ideal and this is your opportunity.

Now, how can you overcome those evil feelings? I advise you to implement RARP and accept that there is nothing you can do to start. Stop trying to hold meetings, stop trying to ask what you can improve on so you can show progress to your coach in order to start, and stop trying to do extra things like clean up all of the team's trash to get noticed by your coach. Just stop. Find peace in the enjoyment of the game, find peace in your own self-development, focus on yourself, increase your probabilities of success in your own position, and find peace in being a pawn in the system. It is all completely out of your control anyway so worrying about it or trying to change your coach's mind is completely futile.

With this mentality, you get to be happy at practice. Because practice is no longer a chance to beat out the starter. It's no longer comparing yourself to another person. It's no longer trying to chase a forever fleeting goal just out of reach. You don't have to be so angry at practice when you make a mistake because that was "your chance to start." You don't have to pray the coach didn't see your error so he doesn't solidify his opinion that you are the inferior player at your position. You don't have to constantly doubt yourself and your skills because you're not starting. It is all out of your control. Practice simply becomes what it used to be. It's a flashback to elementary school when you used to go to soccer practice with your friends and there was no pressure. Practice becomes pure again. It becomes what it's supposed to be: time to have fun with the game you like, time to have fun with your friends, enjoyment of seeing yourself grow as a player, the art of perfecting a craft, the duty to fulfill your commitment to the team, and the ability to be a part of something greater than yourself.

CHAPTER 9

How To Deal With Suddenly And Inexplicably Playing Like Trash

Every athlete has been in this situation. You are inexplicably playing like absolute trash. You feel uncoordinated. You start making errors. You start to worry. A few more errors go by and it feels like it's the first time playing your sport, the sport you've spent tens of thousands of hours mastering. You choke. Then, you start to get embarrassed. I hope my friends, family, crush, or girlfriend are not watching me perform like this. You feel abashed when looking at your teammates or coach and you feel like you're letting them down. Maybe you have a teammate who laments, loudly and to you, that you are playing like trash today. This makes you play even worse. Finally, the sorrow of your situation consumes you. "Why me?" you may ask. Why couldn't you just play perfectly and end the game feeling proud? Instead, you have to finish the game ashamed and feeling like a failure. You go to your room upset. You go to sleep upset. You come to practice the next day with no confidence in your ability. The only remedy comes when you inexplicably and randomly play well again. You feel relieved that your skills have come back to you, forever repeating this cycle.

Sound familiar?

This is the non-RARP way. Notice how everything tied to your ability is almost superstitious and supernatural. Your skill is this foreign spirit that comes and goes as it pleases, out of your control. You desperately call for it to come back, like yelling for a puppy when it runs away. The path to becoming an excellent, high-caliber athlete and PERSON is to stop thinking like this at all costs and incorporate RARP.

There are two main reasons why you make an error. The first reason is that the opponent has done something unexpected/new or is performing at a higher level that you are unpracticed at. The second reason is slightly more complex. You have momentarily developed a negative habit.

REASON 1: THE OPPONENT HAS DONE SOMETHING UNEXPECTED/NEW OR IS PERFORMING AT A HIGHER LEVEL THAT YOU ARE UNPRACTICED AT

During my time at Ship Weight, the best hitter on the team by far was James. James could hit this cross-net cut shot so sharp that it seemed illegal. This mofo would hit the ball so perfectly along the net that it would squeak right under the block, dance across the tape of the net, and then land perfectly on the sideline. If the shot couldn't get any deadlier, James would conceal the intent of his swing so well that I could never really tell when he was going to hit this shot. It always seemed like he was going to pound the ball straight and all of my previous volleyball knowledge told me that he was going to pound the ball straight. I would slide inside to take away his powerful swing, only to be dismayed as I watched that evil cut shot trickle along the net and land on the sideline.

The first time this shot was hit against me I had absolutely no chance of defending it. It was a guaranteed error simply because I had never seen that shot before. It was the same exact way during my time speedrunning Super Smash Bros on the Nintendo 64. If the computer ever did something that I did not have a plan for, the run was over. Guaranteed error. Fortunately, we have a perfect juxtaposition to analyze. When

James was burning me on this shot, I was not implementing RARP, but when I was speedrunning, I was implementing RARP. Note the difference.

For volleyball, the error and aftermath would go as follows. James would hit that cut shot and score against me. He would immediately smack-talk me for not getting the ball. I would get angry that he was smack-talking me, and I would get disappointed in myself for not being a good enough defender to see the shot coming and dig the ball. I would get nervous that the coach would see me fail to get the dig. Then I would think about Kevin's performance and hope he too would make an error so we'd be even on errors. Then the next play would commence.

For speedrunning, the error and aftermath would go as follows. The CPU would move in a new and unexpected way, causing me to error, which killed the run. I would write down this new CPU movement as a category to practice. I would figure out why the CPU moved that way and figure out exactly what to do when he made that move. Once I developed my strategy for that CPU movement, I would practice the strategy until I was satisfied with the probability of my successful completion of said strategy.

To put it into perspective, I could not figure out when James would hit his super cut shot until the end of an entire semester. That is 15 weeks of making the exact same error over and over again. As for speedrunning, I would, at the very least, have a proper strategy and a decent success rate to overcome a new CPU movement after several hours.

The difference is RARP. A critically thinking machine says to itself:

1) I have errored.

2) Why have I errored?

3) Something new happened and I had no strategy.

4) What is the answer to this new problem and how fast can I solve it?

When you don't implement RARP, you are doomed to autopilot. And if you are like me, you autopilot for 15 weeks straight. I was caught up thinking about my own emotions, thinking about if I was playing well, and thinking about what the coach was thinking. I was caught up *worrying about myself*. So much so, that I prevented myself from learning.

You haven't lost your touch and you aren't playing badly. You just need to learn and adapt. Implement RARP so you can. Stop worrying about yourself and your dumb temporary emotions. Stop, critically think, and adapt. The higher up you go in skill at your sport, the more it becomes about adapting. How can I adapt to my opponent adapting to me adapting to his initial adaptation of my technique on the third point of the game? This is the beauty of sports. The puzzle, the out-thinking and trickery, the competition. Allow yourself to get there. Implement RARP.

REASON 2: YOU HAVE MOMENTARILY DEVELOPED A NEGATIVE HABIT

Let us now analyze the second cause of an error. Sports can be incredibly frustrating because we are testing how perfectly and consistently the imperfect human can perform specific actions. Sometimes, your brain just gets the action wrong. Instead of fostering this new bad habit, you have to identify it and fix it right away.

During my competitive Smash Bros esports saga, I remember a specific practice where something strange was happening to me. In Smash Bros, there's a move called B-reversing. It is a very precise move where the player must press the B button and then perfectly time a flick of the control stick in the opposite direction of the character's movement. If the flick comes too early or too late the move will not work. During this practice, I could not B-reverse to save my life. It made no sense. I could B-reverse perfectly fine the last practice, the practice before that, and the ten practices before that! But for whatever reason, I could not do it at this practice and I was losing games because of it.

Instead of getting angry, frustrated, or lamenting that I was "in my head," I strictly thought about what I could do to fix the problem. The only answer that I could come up with was to identify exactly what I was physically doing wrong with my hands. I determined that every time I failed a B-reverse, I was flicking the stick too early. During the next match, I focused on flicking the control stick later than normal and I was immediately back to my normal B-reversing self. I did not fail a B-reverse the rest of the practice.

It's not just video games where this happens. Something similar happened to me just a few months ago (at the time of writing this book) when playing the Orange County Stunners in the National Volleyball Association. I seemingly could not pass a float serve in the beginning of the match. All of my passes were 15 feet off of the net, an undesirable location for the standard of play at this level. I remember immediately thinking that I was "off," that I felt "rusty" and that I was in a "slump." I thought that maybe I was thinking too much and I was too "in my head." But then I caught myself. I was better than this. I implemented RARP and told myself that my body was just a machine performing actions. It was not a mentality or a feeling that was causing the error, it was something my robot body was physically doing that was causing the error. I asked myself, "what is my body doing wrong?" I noticed that my body was too far away from the ball. My coach told me the same thing which cemented my belief that I had located the problem. I focused on stepping closer to the ball on serve receive and I was back to my perfect-passing self.

The mind and body are weird. Sometimes you just develop a negative habit. But that is a main element of being human. If you could perfectly perform every action, sports would be incredibly boring. The battle is against your opponent but it's also against yourself. How quickly can you critically think, adapt, and fix random negative habits that pop up? How fast can you go from faulty superstition about "being in your head" to constructive RARP thinking?

There you have it. Those are the two main reasons why you just made an error and are "inexplicably" underperforming. The truth is that you don't have time to think about how badly you are playing and feeling all of these negative emotions. You only have the duration of the match and you're RUNNING OUT OF TIME. You are in a constant battle of time to out-adapt your opponent. Whoever out-adapts their opponent will win. You must use every second to learn your opponent and mitigate your own errors and random bad habits. You have to use RARP or else you allow your opponent to learn your weaknesses and ultimately win.

A FINAL NOTE ABOUT ERRORS

Remember that a founding principle of RARP is understanding that you are a statistic and that your probability of success is the only truth. Math is the truth. Try not to fall into the trap of misrepresenting random sequences. Allow me to explain. Let's say you are an elite three-point shooter in basketball that has a 40% success rate from the three-point line.

The following are two different scenarios of 20 shots across two games. Let's say you take 10 shots each game. X will represent a missed shot. O will represent a made shot.

Scenario 1:
     Game 1: O O O O O O O O X X
     Game 2: X X X X X X X X X X

Scenario 2:
     Game 1: X O X O X O X O X O
     Game 2: X X O X X O X X O X

In both scenarios, you shot 40% from the three-point line. However, in Scenario 1, after game 2, because you shot zero for ten, you may feel like there is something wrong with you and that you are "in a slump" and "off your game." It is not valuable to view yourself on a game-by-game basis. You must think analytically and view yourself as a long-term machine. By implementing RARP and understanding statistics, you can save yourself from the emotional misery of "having a bad game" and become indifferent to poor moment-in-time performances.

The only thing you can do is critically think and try to come up with a reason for why you missed any shot.

Maybe you find out the error was caused by Reason 1 and your opponent did something strange and new like tap your stomach every time you shot, forcing you to go up differently. Now, during practice, you can emulate this scenario, increase your probability of success when your opponent does this, and thus become a better player.

Maybe you find out the error was caused by a subcategory of Reason 1 and it wasn't the opponent doing something new, but the environment was new. Maybe you were playing on a different surface. Maybe the ball was extra pumped up. Either way, during practice, you can emulate this scenario, increase your probability of success when the environment is like this, and thus become a better player.

Maybe you find out the error was caused by Reason 2 and that you have developed a negative habit like releasing the ball slightly later than you used to. Now, during practice, you can focus on releasing the ball slightly earlier, hammer out that negative habit, and thus become a better player.

Maybe you just missed ten shots in a row and nothing specific was wrong. You were wide open for all of the shots so the opponent didn't do anything new. Also, there was no one specific bad habit that explains why you missed all of the shots. You can't be perfect and shoot 100%. The truth is you are **still on par** with your 40% benchmark even though shots were missed in a row. Therefore, there's nothing wrong, and your only solution is to remain unbothered and keep shooting.

CHAPTER 10

How to Talk To Your Teammates

Teammates are the greatest resource for you to further implement RARP, avoid autopiloting, and adapt. The teams that adapt the fastest to their opponents are usually excellent at communicating with each other. But how do you talk to your teammates during the game? What should you say? What should you talk about? During competition, a lot is going on. One of your teammates is "in his head." Another teammate is pissed and punches a chair. Another teammate is fired up because his hitting percentage is off the charts. Games can be absolute emotional chaos especially because not all of your teammates are RARPing. So how can you be a good teammate and talk to win games?

There is only one rule to follow. You must only talk about strategy.

To better elaborate on this philosophy, allow me to explore types of teammates that are *bad* at communicating so you can avoid becoming these types of players.

THE APOLOGIZER

During a volleyball match, you have roughly 20 seconds in between points to regroup and talk to your teammates before the next serve is entered. Here is a real conversation I had with a teammate in a match

once. The opponent had just gotten a kill on him down the line, shank-
ing the pass high on his right arm. The conversation went like this:

Him: "I'm sorry."
Me: "No worries, it was a good swing. He likes to swi..."
Him: "My bad."
Me: "It's alright. Plenty of game left."
Him: "I'm so lazy. That's an easy dig. My bad."
Me: "It's fine."
Him: "I'm playing so bad."
Me: "No you're not. It's one point."
Him: "My bad."
Me: "It's okay. I think we can get him by shifting our defense to..."
Him: "Sorry."

Reading this conversation seems insane. How could a conversation
like this possibly happen? It's not even a conversation. What's happening here is my teammate is not RARPing. He is stuck in autopilot
and not critically thinking. He is actually so stuck in autopilot that he
cannot even hear what I am saying to him. He is strictly thinking about
his error, and about how embarrassed he is for losing the point. On the
other hand, I am RARPing. I am desperately trying to communicate to
my teammate a way to adapt, so we can dig the ball the next time a play
like this happens. All players have tendencies and will eventually hit the
same attack to the same spot. I wanted to strategize with my teammate
and shift our defense back further and have another player cover the
short ball, that way he would not miss the dig high on his body like
he previously did. But, he was too busy apologizing and auto-piloting,
forcing us to remain locked and stagnant. We literally could not adapt.
We were doomed to error on this same opponent's attack over and over.

Do not apologize for making an error. This is incredibly hard and a
skill I still have yet to master. But really, what is saying sorry going to do
about the error? It does nothing but wastes precious strategizing time.

Do not be The Apologizer. Implement RARP. Talk strategy.

THE COACHER

At Ship Weight, I had a teammate that I particularly disliked. He bullied me constantly and talked about me behind my back, but worst of all, he was The Coacher. The Coacher does not strategize with you but instead commands you. No less than 10,000 times, whenever a ball landed, no matter if it were my fault or not, my teammate would come over to me, instruct me to "BE HERE," point at where the ball landed, and then go back to his position.

He never talked about strategy, how we could read the opponent to predict where the ball would land, or talk about the hitter's tendencies. He only commanded me to stand where the ball just landed. How stupid is that? If I knew where every ball was going to land, I would be the greatest volleyball player in the world and completely break the game. His command of, "just be where the ball will land" was pointless and unhelpful.

I have witnessed another interaction where one player walked over to his teammate after practice and asked him if he "wanted advice." The approached player reluctantly said yes, just to be nice. The approacher then went on a five-minute explanation of why the teammate's serve is bad and how he could fix it by adjusting his entire arm swing. The two left the conversation with clear tension in the air. The approached player was biting his tongue. He desperately wanted to tell his teammate to piss off, that there was nothing wrong with his serve, and that his teammate was a know-it-all for being so sure that there even was a problem and that he had the solution. The approacher left the conversation slightly oblivious, feeling good about himself that he "helped someone."

In short, The Coacher sucks. The Coacher thinks he knows everything and if everyone were just to listen to him, every game would result in victory. He has no problem telling other players what to do, no matter how poorly he is playing. He even has no mercy in critiquing a player's form, a subject that is incredibly subjective and would need an expert (like your coach) to address.

To avoid being The Coacher, never instruct or teach your teammates ever. Never say that they need to do this or command them to do that. You don't have the answer or key to victory. If you think you do, you're wrong. If you think you are the exception, you are very wrong. You hardly know anything. This is why you strategize with your team.

If you think you have a good idea and want to try to adjust the team's strategy, do two things. Always talk in a frame of reference to the opponent and always use the word "we."

Let's look at some examples.

Example 1 (The Opponent Is Doing Something - Easiest)

Let's say your teammate has just hit the ball into the block three times in a row. Unless your teammate is a perfect RARPer, he's going to be a little emotionally shaken (angry, sad, annoyed, confused, whatever). The Coacher will say, "Stop getting blocked!" This is so unhelpful and dumb. Obviously, your teammate wants to stop getting blocked. He's trying. The Coacher might also instruct, "Swing cross!" Even if The Coacher is 100% correct and your teammate does simply need to swing cross, he's not going to hear your advice. He cannot interpret the instruction because he is too distraught by the fact that his own teammate thinks he has the right to tell him what to do. Again, as stated before, the teammate does not have to "toughen up." If you are thinking this, you are wrong. If you think your teammates are soft and need to toughen up, you're probably The Coacher and you suck. It is a completely natural reaction to be hateful, angry, or shocked when a teammate self-promotes and thinks he can tell you what to do (outside of the default rights of the position. ie. a goalie commanding his teammates to push the defensive line for an offsides trap).

To not act like The Coacher, the player needs to tell his blocked teammate something like this, "Hey, that blocker is pretty good. It looks like he's lining up on your cross and then jumping to your line. I think if you give him the ol' body facing line cut back cross, we got him." Notice the frame of reference, the phrase "I think," and the word "we."

The frame of reference is the opponent. It's not, "you are doing this wrong, that is why you are erroring." Instead, it is, "the opponent is doing this well, we must adapt and innovate something new." When you frame it in reference to the player it causes frustration because it puts the responsibility solely on the teammate. You did this wrong. You errored. You suck. You do not want to do this because it forces the player to think about himself and his performance instead of thinking about being a robot, RARPing, and analyzing the game. When you put the communication in the frame of the opponent, the player thinks about the opponent. What is the opponent doing well? This *naturally* causes your teammate to think about the opposing team and thus the game. It forces your teammate to strategize. It's daunting and hard to face a challenge within yourself. It is way easier to face an outside challenge that is approaching you, such as a worthy opponent.

Next, I use the phrase "I think…" Saying that you "think" completely removes any command out of your language. It shows that you are strategizing, not informing. It communicates that you have a plan, you are humble enough to see that it is just a plan, and you do not know if it will work. If you think you know it will work, you are wrong. If you think you are the exception, you are super wrong. Your teammates interpret your idea as a strategy and think about your advice in a critical RARP way. After some debating (or not) your team can accept the strategy and move forward as a team.

Finally, I say "WE got him" at the end. This enforces and reminds the idea that it's not just him getting blocked. We as a team are getting blocked and it's up to us to find a way to not get blocked. This is the definition of a team. It is not you erroring, it is the team erroring. It is not you winning, it is the team winning. It is not you losing, it is the team losing. It is not you scoring, it is the team scoring. Saying "WE" is a reminder of this mentality. It reminds an erroring player that they are not alone and his team has his back, arguably the most comforting feeling in the world. If a player is reminded that it's not just all up to him and he has a team that has his back, he is less likely to lose all confidence and can remain "in the game."

Anytime an opponent is doing something, it is easy to communicate with your teammate. Take two more examples for good measure because this is important.

If a teammate misses a dig, The Coacher will yell, "STAND HERE" or "DIG THAT!" A good teammate will say, "Hey, the opponent seems to hit only the back foot of the court. I think if we stand deep we can dig him." Is the frame of reference in the opponent? Check. Was "I think" used? Check. Was "We" used? Check.

If a teammate gets aced, The Coacher will yell "PASS THE BALL!" A good teammate will say "Hey, looks like the opponent got our line here. I think we should have you protect your line and take a step closer to it. We will manage the rest of the court in case he changes his serving location." Is the frame of reference in the opponent? Check. Was "I think" used? Check. Was "We" used? Check.

Example 2 (The Opponent Did Nothing But Another Teammate Did - Medium)

Some errors cannot be phrased in reference to the opponent. This is especially true when the opponent did nothing to cause your teammate's error. In this case, to avoid being The Coacher, all advice remains the same except for the change of putting the frame of reference on another teammate.

Allow this example. The setter sets the ball too low and your teammate hits the ball into the net. The Coacher will either yell at the setter "SET THE BALL HIGHER" or yell at the hitter "JUST GET IT OVER THE NET!" This advice is pointless, unstrategic, and everyone already knows what The Coacher just yelled. The setter can clearly see his set was too low. The hitter can clearly see he should not have hit the ball into the net. A good teammate would communicate like this, "Hey, it looks like the set from our setter was a little low. I think when that happens, the deep corner is open. We can score this way." Again, I took the frame of reference off of the teammate I am communicating with and put it on the other teammate's set instead. My teammate is now thinking outside of himself and about the game which is the point of strategizing. I still use "I think" and "we" for the same reasons.

An important note is that you are not completely blaming the other teammate and throwing him under the bus. You are just stating a fact about what another teammate is doing and how to adapt to the teammate's actions. I said our setter set the previous ball low. I did not say our setter is playing terribly to another teammate. Do not instill anger and hatred among teammates by talking negatively about them to other teammates.

Example 3 (The Opponent Nor Another Teammate Did Anything - Hardest)

The hardest scenario is when your teammate makes an unassisted error. No opponent or teammate was involved in the play, just the teammate who made the error. Allow this example. Your teammate serves the ball out of bounds. The Coacher will yell, "JUST PUT THE SERVE IN" or, infinitely worse, will start teaching and say something like, "you dropped your arm on that serve and that's why it didn't go over." The problem with yelling "JUST PUT THE SERVE IN" is that it's a no-duh statement. The Coacher added no value to the situation and probably just pissed off the server a little more if he is not RARPing. The Coacher teaching how to serve is more problematic. The Coacher makes two major faults by teaching. First, he self-promotes, which infers he believes he has more importance than other players and can rise from his pawn status. Second, by teaching, he believes he is infallibly correct with no room for debate. It doesn't even matter if his teaching is correct, these are still scary fundamental flaws in thought by The Coacher that your real coach should address but won't.

Here is what you should say. In this case, probably nothing. But, if you *really* think it will help your team's chances of winning, say this, "Hey, I think the ball caught us a little low on your serve. What do you think?" The frame of reference is *still* not on the teammate. The frame of reference is the ball, ensuring the teammate is thinking outside of himself and about the game. I still use the word "us" even though he is the only one serving to remind him to think of errors as a team issue. Finally, I use "I think" in combination with asking him what he saw on his own serve to ensure the discussion of strategy occurs and to show (and remind myself) that I may be completely wrong.

Do not be The Coacher. Implement RARP. Talk strategy.

THE SULKER

Negativity is a more powerful emotion than positivity, unfortunately. Negativity can destroy the mood of any group, and that truth is no different for teams in the middle of a game. The Sulker is one who complains about the current situation. If you are losing, The Sulker will whine and moan about the score. If you are tied, the sulker will lament the fact that the team should be winning. If the sulker makes an error, he will be visibly sad and mope back to his position. Here is a real conversation I had with a roommate who was The Sulker when we were playing the baseball video game, Mario Super Sluggers, on the Wii. It was the top of the second of nine innings and we were down one run. We were pitching against the computers.

Roommate: "I can't believe we are losing."
Me: "It's all good. Plenty of game left. We got this."
Roommate: "No, we shouldn't be losing. We should just start over."
Me: "I mean... we could but I don't feel like picking teams again. Let's just stop 'em here and score big at our at bat."
Roommate: "We made the computers too hard. Let's just start over."
Me: "What? These computers are a bunch of chumps. We got DK and King K Rool on our team! We literally can't lose!"
Roommate: "No this is embarrassing. I don't wanna do this."

I love Mario Super Sluggers and it is really hard for me not to have fun while playing this game. But, dear lord, I had zero amount of fun playing the game with The Sulker. Maybe my roommate was an extreme case of The Sulker, but still, I see versions of The Sulker all the time in volleyball.

The Sulker is a non-RARPer. He feels negative emotions like a human, and even worse, outwardly expresses them to his teammates. He's a captain on a sinking ship and drags his crew down with him. He removes himself from thinking critically about the game, and like an invisible disease, spreads it to his teammates. The Sulker sucks the fun out of the game for his teammates and pushes them to lament that he is lamenting about the game.

Just like The Apologizer's apologies, The Sulker's sad and negative talk adds no value to the game and does not increase your team's probabilities of success. There is a task at hand which is to out-adapt and beat your opponent. Being sad that the task exists will not help. Being sad that you are failing at completing the task (losing the game) will not help either. What is being sad about the previous errors that have led to your team's current losing status going to do? Nothing. What does outwardly expressing this sadness do? Even worse than nothing.

Do not be The Sulker. Implement RARP. Talk strategy.

THE RAGER

Anger is blinding. It takes over your body and prevents you from thinking clearly. It is a primal fight instinct designed to defend yourself in life-or-death scenarios. In the caveman days, while defending your family from a predator, I'm sure anger was incredibly valuable. Unfortunately, that same value does not carry over to the volleyball court after you make an error.

I've seen it thousands of times before. The Rager makes an error. He rages. He punts a ball in frustration. He yells at himself. He clenches his fists. He screams. He then makes the same error over and over. I know this because I was the Rager in my Super Smash Bros esports days. Remember what I learned, the Rager is forever doomed to autopilot.

Whenever I see The Rager as my opponent, I try to get him the ball. No person is more obviously autopiloting than The Rager. A person that autopilots takes the same swing over and over and never adapts. I always strategize with my blocker to block The Rager in his line of approach because he is not thinking and is just trying to hit the ball straight and as hard as he can. He is going to swing where he is most comfortable (in his line of approach) and then get blocked. We will then serve him again and block him again because he is not adapting due to his anger.

The Rager is out of control. He yells at his teammates for making errors, makes big exasperated expressions when he does not get the ball, pouts, and stomps around. This type of communication alienates him from his team as no one can logically and safely communicate with him. Not only that, The Rager puts all of his teammates on edge. No teammate wants to make an error because there is a fear of being met with a verbal (or nonverbal) negative and angry repercussion. This makes The Rager's teammates play tentative, scared, uninspired, and safe. Playing this way leaves no room for creativity, the foundation for adaptation, thus lowering the team's overall probability of winning.

I have seen many players attempt to implement rage into their performance. Rage feels good due to the fieriness. It can help you hit the ball harder, move faster, and be more aggressive. But the momentary benefits do not outway the inevitable con of autopiloting, which is failure.

Do not be The Rager, especially if someone is egging you on to be The Rager. Smack talk is a real strategy to force your opponent into becoming The Rager. By forcing the opponent to become The Rager, even momentarily, the opponent has become more predictable due to autopiloting and his team becomes weakened due to uninspired and safe play because of fear. Do not fall for smack talk. Implement RARP, analyze if the words have any value, and disregard them if they don't.

Do not be The Rager. Implement RARP. Talk strategy.

THE ENCOURAGER

Encouragement can be good but it is no replacement for strategy. The Encourager only encourages and never talks about strategy. He only says uplifting statements. He only reassures everyone. He strictly celebrates during the good and tries to calm everyone during the bad. The Encourager may seem good and certainly does not harm as much as the Rager or Sulker. However, The Encourager still harms because he stifles strategy and debate.

Take this example inspired by multiple experiences I had with many Encouragers over the years of playing volleyball. Let's say I was just blocked by my opponent and lost the point.

Me: "Hey setter. Good set, he got me…."
Setter: "It's okay."
Me: "Yeah for sure. I wanna try moving my set…"
Setter: "We'll get the next one."
Me: "I'm sure. So this guy's a good blocker and…"
Setter: "That's okay. You got him. Just keep playing your game! Stay positive."
Me: "Yeah… I know… I want my set closer to the pin!"
Setter: "No worries. We got this."

Again, reading the conversation on paper, your initial thought is probably that there is no way communication looks like this. I promise you, when players are auto-piloting, not RARPing, and not critically thinking, it really does go like this. The Encourager is too focused on "mentally resetting" that he has completely forgotten to strategize and adapt. Even though these words may sound comforting, they lose their appeal after hearing them after every single lost point. It is not enough to get to the next point. You have to adapt. In the conversation above I wanted to move my set around so I could overcome the good blocker. Unfortunately, it did not seem like my message was received because The Encourager was not critically thinking.

Do not be The Encourager. Implement RARP. Talk strategy.

THE SPIRITUALIST

The Spiritualist attributes anything and everything to a non-specific cause. He will never talk about strategy but only talk about feelings. The Spiritualist speaks in cliches and his words have no actual meaning. Instead of critically thinking about the game and talking about details, he will speak about everything extremely abstractly.

I personally have never encountered The Spiritualist midgame. The Spiritualist usually comes out during the post-game analysis or in a timeout. Here is a real conversation I had with a teammate after losing a match:

Me: "Hey teammate. Tough one. How did we lose that? What were they doing that was so good?"

Teammate: "I don't know man. They just balled up and we didn't."

Me: "Right... yeah. But was it our siding out (offense) or defense that was the problem?"

Teammate: "I think they were just more confident than us and played their game."

Me: "Cool... but did we get blocked too much? Did we not dig enough balls? Where did we lose our points?"

Teammate: "They just stepped up to the plate and were feeling themselves. They were in flow and we were nervous. We didn't play our game and it just wasn't our day."

Me: "Alright."

What on earth was my teammate even saying? Seriously, he said so many words and none of them had any meaning. My teammate was The Spiritualist. When you lose, you lose for a specific, real reason. The other team scored more points than you. Why? Because they had more digs and more blocks. Because they tricked us by dive-blocking and we didn't adapt. Maybe the reason is complex or maybe the reason is simple, but you did not lose because the stars weren't aligned or because a higher being didn't want you to. You lost because of something that physically happened in the game, and it's your job to find it so you can adapt for the next game.

I cannot stand The Spiritualist. If I hear the words "we didn't play our game" one more time, I'm going to uppercut a baby chicken. The Spiritualist distracts you from real strategizing and prevents you from learning from mistakes, which is the catalyst for becoming a better player. The Spiritualist will keep making the same errors over and over because he never identifies why the error actually happened!

Do not be The Spiritualist. Implement RARP. Talk strategy.

THE TWO STAGES A PLAYER CAN BE IN DURING A GAME

As previously stated, the goal of talking to your teammates is always to talk about the game and find ways you can adapt to beat your opponent. However, sometimes this is impossible depending on what stage your teammate is in. A teammate can be in two stages. Bad stage: He is emotionally distressed and cannot talk strategy. Good stage: He is emotionally sound and can talk strategy. A RARPer is always in the good stage, never emotionally distressed, and always available and ready to talk and debate strategy. However, not everyone is RARPing. If your teammate is in the bad stage, you must first pull him out of the bad stage before you can talk strategy with him. Attempting to talk strategy with someone in the bad stage is futile. They are not thinking about the game and will not register your words. There are a few strategies I have found to effectively pull someone out of the bad stage.

My favorite technique is the fun reminder technique. This technique reminds your teammate that you are simply playing a game and that it is just for fun. It brings them back to their root for playing. It brings them back in touch with their core (more on that in the chapter How To Deal With Being Lost, Burnt Out, or Late-Stage Pessimistic). The implementation of this technique is very simple. All you have to do is ask your teammate, "are you having fun?" while they are in the bad stage. The question is most effective when asked immediately after your teammate's error.

This question can have successful results in multiple ways. Most times, the absurdity of being asked if you're having fun immediately after making an error will cause your teammate to laugh. A laugh is excellent, it pulls your teammate out of sadness or anger and can be a great reset out of the bad stage. If your teammate doesn't laugh and remains stuck in seriousness, anger, sadness, and the land of autopiloting, the question may linger around in his brain. Maybe in a few points, he will ask himself, "hmm, why aren't I having fun?" He will then logic out an answer, "because I am losing." Then, hopefully, he will ask "why am I losing?" which is back to the good stage of critically thinking about the game. Sometimes, and my personal favorite response, your teammate will answer that he is not having fun. He will then try to explain why he is not having fun playing the sport he has fun playing. He will try to logic through and explain this obvious contradiction, be unable to because it is a contradiction, realize that what he is trying to argue is foolish, and be reset by the hilarity and absurdity of the situation.

Another technique is the cry for help technique. This technique reminds your teammate that he is a member of a team and has a responsibility to strategize with his teammates. To implement this technique, tell your teammate, "hey, it's okay, I need you to win this game. Help me." This comment can be valuable because it forces your teammate to stop thinking about just himself. In the bad stage, a player only thinks about his own errors and his own performance. Sometimes a simple, "I need your help" forces your teammate to think "how can I help my teammate?" This question will logically lead to your teammate asking himself how he can improve his play to help his teammate and team. This is the good stage and your teammate is ready to strategize.

A third technique is the full support technique. Sometimes, the previous technique might push your teammate further into the bad stage. Instead of thinking of how he can help his teammate after the cry for his help, he may become disheartened that he is letting his team down. If you notice your teammate responds in this manner or you feel he may be likely to respond in this manner, the full support technique may be more effective.

The full support technique also reminds your teammate he is a member of a team. But, instead of bolstering him through the reminder of responsibility, you bolster him through the reminder of family. To implement the technique, say something along the lines of, "hey, it's okay. I got you. I'll score the next point for us. Let me lift you up and take some weight. You've been carrying a lot so far." This may release some anxiety and pressure off of your teammate, removing him from the bad stage and pushing him toward the good stage.

A fourth technique is the long game technique. This technique reminds your teammate that there is a lot of game left and everything does not have to be solved in the next point. The implementation looks like this, "hey, I know it's game point for the opponent, but there is still a lot of game left. Let's get on a run." This comment can pull your teammate out of despair and hopelessness. The idea is to stop any negative feelings of premature loss (bad stage) and instill the idea that there is still a job to do, work to be done, and time to invent and adapt. Since there is still time left, it forces the question of what still needs to be done in order to win (good stage). This technique is more effective than one might realize. My brother, Dylan, instilled this technique in me. When we play video games together, and I am down on my luck against a tough boss, he always reminds me "you can do a lot on one life." It always pulls me out of the bad stage. It doesn't matter if I lost all my lives in dumb ways before, I have this life, and there is plenty of time to make this one work.

Maybe all of these techniques work for all of your teammates. Maybe none of them work for any of your teammates. But the truth is that your teammates cannot talk strategy in the bad stage. You need to talk strategy to win and avoid autopiloting. You need your teammates to win. You know your teammates better than I do. Maybe you have more techniques, a funny phrase, a cool handshake, or a witty rib. Use them so your team can RARP and talk strategy. Keep in mind though that some teammates (maybe most) cannot be helped. Do not let that affect you. A negative teammate is far worse than a taunting opponent. How effectively can you implement RARP to not let teammates' negativity affect you?

CHAPTER 11

How To Deal With Seniority

Seniority is fundamentally flawed and the antithesis of the philosophy of a team. Because your coach sucks at his job, he probably will let seniority run untethered, instilling chaos into the structure of your team.

Seniority is the fraudulent use of nonexistent power. It is when a pawn or group of pawns self-promote on the account of age, an arbitrary and uncontrollable characteristic, in order to gain perks. It is a cheap trick that is easily implemented, especially when the team has a majority of upperclassmen. You are on one of two sides of this coin. The one in power, or the one not in power.

Before we explain what to do in each situation, we must first examine why seniority is fundamentally flawed. At Ship Weight, during my third year, I debated with a fifth-year teammate about why I thought seniority is stupid. We were both upper-classmen at this point and I was trying to convince him to give up his perks so we could put an end to the endless cycle of seniority. He argued that seniority was fair. He said that he had "done his time" as an underclassman and can now reap the benefits. It's perfectly fair because the work evens out - extra work the first two years, no work the second two.

This explanation seems to be fair but it is flawed because it examines work too abstractly. In a mutual agreement involving work, there are two parties. The first party works for the second party and the second party rewards the first party for the work. In other words, the rewarder is indebted to the worker as a fundamental principle of the agreement. If I paint a picture for a client, the client will pay me. I worked for the client and the client rewarded me. The client was indebted to me for my work due to the agreement. When a child does his chores for the week, he may get McDonald's from his parents as a reward. The child worked for the parent and the parent rewarded the child. The parent was indebted to the child for the work due to the agreement. There is a one-to-one reward for work. In any mutual agreement such as the previously mentioned scenarios, *the rewarder is indebted to the worker.*

With seniority, the idea of the rewarder being indebted to the worker is nonexistent, therefore there is no mutual agreement. If you break seniority down further, it really becomes absurd. With seniority, the 18-year-old freshman is the worker and the future player of the college, a 16-year-old high school kid who does not even know what school he is going to, is the rewarder. With the logic of seniority, a 16-year-old, in some random place in the world becomes indebted to a freshman because the freshman did work in some other random place in the world. A person has become indebted to another person and they have not even met. Does this make any sense? Of course not. That is the equivalent of me painting a picture for a client and going up to a stranger and demanding he pays me because I did a good job. Absolutely ludicrous. This makes me question, is the random 16-year-old really the rewarder in the agreement? He is not because the members of a mutual agreement are the ones involved with each other. The real mutual agreement occurring is much darker, uglier, and twisted.

When analyzed, seniority cannot be hidden under the guise of fairness, even though generations of people have tried. So what is actually happening with seniority? Why do underclassmen even agree to do chores if it makes absolutely no sense? It's because they *are* being rewarded by the upperclassmen. They are being rewarded with social peace, friendship, and acceptance. What happens if the underclassmen refuse to do the chores? They are met with discord, ostracization, and bullying.

Seniority is not an agreement.

It's a threat.

THE ONE NOT IN POWER

You are an underclassman and on the wrong side of the coin. Not only do you have to deal with a new school, a new coach, new teammates, a new roommate, and new responsibilities that come with your new freedom, you must also deal with constantly being threatened by your upperclassmen. Somehow you must deal with being threatened by your own teammates.

If you recall from my story at Ship Weight, I went to war with the encouragement (and no support) of my coach. I fought them to the death on every aspect of their enforcement of seniority. From setting up the net, to getting water, to being last in line for food, to hosting recruits, to doing all the work for fundraisers, to being pranked, to being hazed, I had something to say. I tried everything from ignoring them, confronting them, disobeying their instruction, debating them, and telling the coach. It was all completely futile. Do not go to war because you will lose. You cannot fight multiple people, nor can you change the status quo forcefully. If you think you are the exception, you are wrong. The only person that can forcefully change the status quo and eliminate seniority is the one person in power, your coach. If seniority is in effect, your coach already knows about it and doesn't care. If you do not believe that sentence, you are a fool.

So what should you do? Again, we must go back to RARP and focus on ourselves. You cannot control that seniority is present. You cannot control the removal of seniority. You cannot assist your coach in the removal of seniority. It's just you. Imagine seniority as being lost in the woods by yourself. You cannot control being lost in the woods. You are simply there. The only thing you can control is surviving.

For any high-level seniority offense, go above your coach and find help. High-level seniority offenses include being forced to be urinated on in the shower, being forced to binge drink, being physically assaulted, being inhumanly humiliated, or being hazed. Really anything that involves you personally and supersedes doing menial tasks in the realm of your sport is a high-level seniority offense. When I was jumped by my teammates, I should have called the police. No question about it. But, I was so stuck in the realm of my school and my team, I didn't think to seek help outside of that realm. Go to the police. Go to the athletic director. Go to the president of the school. In these scenarios, you must have no mercy and call attention to the evil.

For any low-level seniority offense, just do the command without resistance. Low-level seniority offenses include getting the water, setting up the net, getting food last, and any other dumb, small perk the upperclassmen want out of laziness. It may seem lame to simply give in to the upperclassmen and be treated like a slave. But your goal is not pride, it's survival. And to survive, you must lay low. You are simply biding your time until you become an upperclassman.

THE ONE IN POWER

You are an upperclassman on the right side of the coin. If you continue using seniority to gain perks, you are threatening the underclassmen. Do not let anyone convince you that seniority is harmless because they are dead wrong. There is no gray area. There is no "oh well the freshmen seem okay with it" or "the underclassmen don't hesitate to do what I say, so it's okay" or "I did my time so it's only fair." You cannot rationalize a threat. Threatening innocent freshmen is wrong. Seniority is wrong. You can either continue being an evil person that threatens his teammates with no merit or you can make a change.

How can you make this change? Again, you cannot forcefully take over the status quo of your team and eliminate seniority. You do not have the power. We must understand RARP and conclude we can only control ourselves. To make the change you have to sacrifice for the freshmen. You must overcorrect to fight seniority. You need to be a servant to the freshmen. If seniority says the freshmen get their food last, you are at the back of the line. If seniority says the freshmen must get the waters for the team, you get the waters. If seniority says the freshmen must set up the net, you set up the net.

Your goal is not to change the rest of the upperclassmen. They will probably stick to the status quo and enforce seniority because most people are unheroic and lazy. Your goal is to conduct yourself in a morally right manner. Hopefully, by being so helpful and such an excellent role model to a freshman, he will become like you when he is an upperclassman. With luck, he will feel the responsibility of helping the underclassmen instead of exploiting them due to your guidance via your actions. Then, over generations, as this continues, seniority may disappear by itself and you can find value in being a pawn that helped the system, the job you signed up to do. If you make that impact, great. If you don't, oh well, it's out of your control.

CHAPTER 12

How To Deal With Disappointment In The Team Culture

If you have a good coach he will explicitly set the team culture. He will lay out exact and clear rules of how to behave, how to dress, how to speak, when to speak, and how to exist. You can tell when a coach has clearly defined the culture because there is no confusion. Here are two examples.

I am not sure why, but I see well-established cultures in basketball the most often. In middle school, I played against a team in basketball that whenever one of their players hit the floor, the entire team would sprint over to him and contend to be the one to help him up. This wasn't naturally established by the players. It was clear the coach set a cultural rule - if your teammate is on the floor, run over and help him up.

For my Professional Team, The New Jersey Freedom, in the National Volleyball Association, recently we lost our semi-final match. During the match, one of our teammates became frustrated with our current losing situation and refused to come into the huddle in between a point. Our coach immediately pulled him from the game. He was playing excellently but it did not matter. The rules of our team culture were clear and there were clear repercussions for not following them.

The establishment of team culture can be little things too. If the coach cares about punctuality, then anyone who shows up late will be sent home and unable to practice. If your coach cares about the look and feel of the team, then anyone who shows up in the wrong practice jersey will be sent home and unable to practice. This is what a good coach does. He has rules and enforces the rules no matter what.

Your coach is probably not like this. He has rules but does not enforce them. If one player wants to do something that goes against the team culture your coach is wishy-washy and allows it. Your coach makes arbitrary exceptions to his own rules. Your coach doesn't explicitly state the rules so there is confusion. Your coach yells at you for not following a rule you did not know existed, building resentment. Your coach allows players to randomly provide input for what the culture should be. Your coach allows the players to try to define the culture through democracy which is always an absolute trainwreck.

Since your coach has not defined the team culture or does not enforce the team culture (virtually the same thing) there will be disastrous repercussions for you and your teammates. The problem will always perfectly come to light in the all-too-treacherous player-led practice. If the undefined team culture is the dynamite, then the player-led practice is the spark. Here's how this explosion goes.

Your coach runs out of usable coaching hours in adherence to the NCAA rules and regulations. To circumnavigate this (foolish already) he allows a player-led practice that is "optional." Intense emphasis on the quotation marks around optional. Usually, you are not really sure if it's optional or not. Legally it's optional because the coach cannot enforce your attendance without violating the NCAA rules. But what happens when the coach finds out you weren't at the optional practice? Do you get punished by not starting? I don't know and neither do you because your coach never defined it. So you have to go anyway making it not optional.

You show up to this player-led practice and your captain has a made-up, half-cooked schedule consisting of drills he liked back in high school. He spends 15 minutes trying to organize this drill and make teams while several players are talking over him and goofing around. He finally manages to get the drill going but it falters and devolves because there is no coach there to enter balls into the drill. He tries to manage the drill while being in it but the whole thing craps out into chaos. After the drill trips its way across the finish line, your captain completely abandons his plan and lamely informs everyone to play 3v3 king of the court (pickup games).

At this point, the clash of cultures is at its highest peak. Your captain is annoyed with certain players for goofing off and not taking things seriously. Some teammates are mad at the captain for not having more control over the team. Some players are annoyed that there even is a practice. Other players are annoyed at the captain for trying too hard and not making the practice just about fun. Some players want the practice to be a relaxing one. Some players want it to be intense. One player has snuck away and is hiding in the locker room. Another one took a 20-minute drink break. Some players are not diving for any ball and trying at 40%. Another player is playing with his shirt off because it's too hot in the gym. It is absolute chaos.

On some teams, the chaos stays at that level. The practice is an absolute wash after 20 minutes. The practice simply ends early and everyone goes home feeling unfulfilled. For other teams, however, it may be worse. Certain players start fighting with each other. "Why aren't you trying?" "Don't tell me what to do, tryhard!" Now you have two players trying to hit the ball as hard as they can at each other, using the practice and sport as a physical fight.

At Ship Weight, I will never forget the player-led practice where we played handball during my freshmen year. The practice was led by an alumnus who came in to facilitate a game that was purposefully not volleyball. The point of the practice was to boost coordination and reaction time or something like that. I don't know, it was odd, and I'm pretty sure the coach did not know what the practice was for either. Anyway, this handball game was so out of control I was fearful for my well-being. The game was being used as an attack against anyone who was disliked on the team. If you recall, the upperclassmen despised me. I was hacked, fouled, taunted, argued with, and clearly targeted. Neither the alumnus nor the coach was calling fouls. I remember once the game was over I went to the locker room and hid for five minutes to recollect myself. It was awful. That may sound cowardly and lame but I was 18 against 22-year-olds. They were way more powerful than me and there was evil intent. They were authentically trying to "rough me up."

At best an undefined culture leads to stagnancy and laziness. At worst it leads to hatred, evil, and malice.

YOU ARE NOT THE SAVIOR

As mentioned before in How To Deal With Seniority, you can not forcefully take over the culture. It is impossible for you, at any year in your collegiate career, to direct and shape the culture into what you want. At Ship Weight, I tried to single-handedly change the culture of the team and I failed. Not only did I fail, I made the time at my school incredibly more complex and difficult. You have to implement RARP and accept what you cannot control. Accept that if your coach does not establish or enforce the culture, your team's culture will be that of laziness and lackadaisical effort. You have to accept that. You cannot change that. Only your coach can change that. No amount of team speeches, extra individual role modeling, or conversations with teammates will change that. If you think you can change your team's culture you are wrong. If you think you are the exception you are so ungodly wrong. Not only are you so mega extra wrong, you are setting yourself up for extra difficulty and sadness for no reason.

The above paragraph might be hard to swallow. I know if I told my 18-year-old self that the team's culture was shot and there was no way of reviving it, I would not believe myself. I would call myself unheroic and even if I couldn't make a difference I would have to try because it would be the right thing to do. I get that. And that is very honorable. But it simply is not your job. Remember you are a pawn. You do not have the power to change the culture, it is not your job to change the culture, and it is wrong to self-promote and declare it your responsibility to change the culture. I should have never tried to change the culture of the Ship Weight Men's Volleyball Team.

When you understand the truth that the team's culture is unchangeable and there is nothing you can do about it, you start to focus on yourself. You initiate RARP, and do the best you can do. You start to think like this:

"I understand my team culture is trash. I understand that our probability of winning is lower because of it. What can I do to increase our probability of winning in a different department? Which department can I control? I can control myself. What is the weakest part of my game and how can I fix it?"

Boom, you are in peak RARP mode again.

It is the same logic as when I was speedrunning video games. I cannot control which way the enemies move just like you cannot control the team culture. Just like you, I could only alter the probabilities of successfully completing my actions.

Don't do what I did and lament and put so much effort into something out of your control. I spent countless hours wishing my team took volleyball more seriously, didn't drink alcohol on the bus on the way back from away games, didn't drink during the week, tried harder at practice, was nicer to each other, had more fun while playing, and weren't so negative. I whined and complained about how the coach was weak, didn't control the players, didn't create a winning culture, didn't discipline any wrongdoing, and rewarded bad behavior. Do you know what all that did for me? Nothing. Actually, worse than nothing. I wasted time. Instead of enjoying my school to the maximum and spending that extra time playing video games and making friends, I spent it being sad on the phone with my parents.

College is precious, even if you don't understand that now. Implement RARP and don't be burdened by things you cannot control, especially your team culture.

CHAPTER 13

How To Deal With Being Lost, Burnt Out, Or Late-Stage Pessimistic

It is perfectly natural to become burnt out. You are performing the same actions over and over, every day. This can drive anyone a little mad. Burnout can happen at any stage. It can happen to a freshman who is overwhelmed with the new responsibility of playing collegiate volleyball. It can also happen to a senior who develops late-stage pessimism and is just simply over it and fed up with playing. Maybe you're burnt out and you don't even know it. Do you dread going to every practice? Do you feel like team lift is a mega chore where you can barely get yourself to move weight? Are you sluggish and half-heartedly playing? Do you have to remind yourself to try at practice? If so, you're probably burnt out.

Burnout is alarming because many players treat this as a sign to quit their sport. Things aren't going your way, you don't really feel like moving, you're not having as much fun as you used to, you're not playing as well, and then all of a sudden, the sport you were in love with is suddenly on the chopping block. You might start telling yourself that maybe it's time to quit. Maybe you've outgrown the sport. I know I've been there.

In my experience, I noticed that the root of feeling burnt out is the loss of purpose. For some reason, the loss of purpose is like the kryptonite of the human spirit. Nothing is more soul-crushing and destroying than being in a position where you feel that your existence is completely pointless. So, in order to alleviate yourself from being burnt out, you have to reconnect with the purpose behind why you play your sport. There are three ways to do this.

RECONNECT 1: IT'S JUST A GAME

You've come a long way since your first time playing the sport. In order to be playing at the collegiate level, you probably have been playing your sport for a long time. You've played in super competitive leagues, gone through extensive training, moved clubs, had private lessons, cried at practice, cried at games, yelled in triumph, won many tournaments, gotten yellow cards, been benched, been the starter, and experienced infinitely more highs and lows. You've really been through a lot with your sport. Not only have you experienced tons of events, but your reasons for playing have also been all over the place too. You've played to get into college, to get a scholarship, to make your dad proud, to win this tournament, to get recruited, to get to a better club, to prove those who doubted you wrong, and infinitely more.

But if you go way back to the first and second times you played, the reason for playing was because it was fun. Sometime long ago, you played your sport because it was just plain fun and you got to hang out with your friends. At some point, your sport was just a game that your parents signed you up for or that you played in the neighborhood. You came back to this game because you thought it was fun.

You need to reconnect to this feeling and this logic. Because behind all of the garbage, the mental anguish, the angry coaches, the "important" matches, the rankings, the starters, the nonstarters, the techniques, the game plans, the frustrations, the pressure, the rituals, the dreams, your sport is just a game that you play for *fun*. We forget that. Your purpose for playing your sport really is that simple. Go to practice because your sport is fun and you get to hang out with your friends. Go to your match and stop feeling this made-up pressure. It's just a game. Laugh on the court, joke with your teammates, joke about the errors, and smile.

But wait, Ryan! You told me to laugh, joke, and smile! Robots don't do these things! RARP is a philosophical tool to clear your mind of the *negative* emotions that drive you to mental chaos and anguish. RARP puts you in a place of mental homeostasis *so* you can enjoy the positive emotions that your sport brings you. RARP frees you *so* you can laugh, joke, smile, and have fun with your sport and your pursuit of completing the challenge of collegiate athletics.

There is purpose in enjoying life through companionship and games. You'll be amazed at how quickly your burnout fades when you remember it's all just a game for fun.

RECONNECT 2: THE PRIDE IN IMPROVEMENT

Have you ever seen someone go through a weight loss journey? Maybe he starts out overweight and unhealthy. Then, little by little, he works out, eats better, and tracks his progress. Then, after several months of dedication, he has transformed into this new person and has found immense pride in himself. There is purpose in self-improvement and you can tap into this to eliminate burnout.

It can be really easy to stop implementing RARP and stop thinking about your performance percentages. All of a sudden you are no longer critically analyzing how you can improve your probabilities of success for individual actions. You just show up to practice, do the same drills over and over, and then go home. It can get boring, monotonous, and drive you straight into burnout. You have to reinvest in analyzing your self-improvement. Even if you don't feel like doing this. Even if you feel it's arbitrary. Reinvest anyway.

To reinvest, first, appreciate how much better you have gotten since you arrived at your college. The high school version of yourself would be amazed at how good you have become. If you think you have gotten worse since you arrived at college, you are wrong. It's nearly impossible.

You are playing higher competition, learning new strategies, and training better optimizations of your body to obtain higher probabilities of success. If you went back now to play at your high school or club you would be surprised at how slow the game is moving and you would wreck kids.

After appreciating how much you have improved, admit that there's plenty more room to grow (even if you are a senior). Implement RARP. Find out what your weakest probabilities are and improve them. Work steadily, a little at a time every day. If you commit to improving, or simpler yet, commit to noticing that you are improving, you can find great purpose and happiness in your growth. With great purpose from the pride of improvement comes the alleviation of burnout.

RECONNECT 3: HELPING OTHERS

No path to finding purpose is shorter than the one of helping others. It is a cheat code of the human spirit. If you are ever lost or feel like you have no purpose, when in doubt, just help someone. This is especially valuable advice if you are a senior as you will naturally have underclassmen looking up to you for guidance.

If you are a senior, your time in the franchise that you bought into is coming to a close. It was already not about you because you are a pawn. Now, it is especially not about you because you are a pawn that the system is about to retire. If you're bored, not feeling it, not having as much fun as before - who cares, it's not about you. Tap into the higher calling of being the hero for those who look to you for guidance. If you think no one looks to you for guidance, you are wrong. You would be surprised just how much information can be gathered for a freshman just by looking at how you behave. Don't turn into The Coacher and don't give yourself managerial responsibilities to take care of the freshmen. Just know that you are being watched like a How-To video on how to act. You can simply be selfish and act lazy because you're not feeling it, or you can find purpose in being a guiding light and shed your burnt-out feelings.

If you are younger in the system, like a freshman, you can still find purpose in helping others. This does not mean kissing up to the upperclassman and perpetuating evil seniority. This means taking pride in doing your job well. If you are feeling burnt out, it is very likely that many others are too. Show up to practice and overcome that feeling because your teammates need you to be there as much as you need them. If you allow the burnout to get to you and show up to practice flat, the effect is more extreme than you think. You become The Sulker with your body language and drag your friends and teammates down. Instead of becoming the Sulker, find purpose in doing your job well to give inspiration and energy to your peers.

Should You Transfer or Quit?

I believe most athletes ask themselves this question. This question arises especially if you are not starting, you don't like your coach, you don't get along with the team, you feel stagnant, your team's losing, or you feel like you're "getting worse." In general, when things are not going your way, this question is bound to reveal itself.

It's not an illogical question. When your circumstances are not what you want them to be, it is a perfectly natural idea to find new circumstances. However, I think both quitting and transferring are two bad options. Let's break down each one.

TRANSFERRING

There are infinitely many reasons to transfer as a student and I am unable to address all of them nor do I want to. I cannot speak for topics such as the quality of your education, financial circumstances, going pro, or family situations that might bolster arguments for transferring. However, I can address the desire to transfer due to dissatisfaction with your team and sport.

When you think about transferring you fall into the trap of wishful thinking. You may think that if you go to a different school, your circumstances will change. You believe things like "if only I had a different coach" or "if only I had teammates who cared." I *promise* you, it's bad all over. I am writing a book for all collegiate athletes containing a line that says "your coach probably sucks at his job" because it applies to the whole country and I'm *not* exaggerating. If you think that you are unfortunate for having the coach you have now and that if you transfer, the chance of getting two bad coaches in a row is low - think again. I argue it is so likely you will have another bad coach that it is almost guaranteed!

Looking back to what we already discussed, a bad coach means no defined culture, which means chaos among the team, which means you'll have all of the same problems as you did before just with different faces and different names.

The truth is that the problem isn't because you are in a specific location. The problem does not reside within your team. The problem is collegiate athletics. The problem is the combination of bad coaches, 18-year-olds not knowing what they signed up for, and the juxtaposition of being treated like an adult while also still being a kid. The problem is the situation. Each new generation of athletes, no matter where they are in the country, will face this war. It's literally a part of growing up. If you transfer, you'll be fighting the same war, just with a slightly different flavor in a battle that's at a different zip code.

You might indeed get lucky or ensure some of your problems disappear. For example, let's say you are in a very tough conference and do not play. You then transfer to a less competitive school and become a starter. Great, now you do not have to worry about sitting the bench (unless they get a superstar freshman next year!). Maybe this new school also has a more family environment and a less corporate environment because they are so small and remote like your high school. Great, now you can be comfortable again with the environment you were used to as a kid.

But there is something impure about abandoning a problem by changing circumstances to obtain comfort instead of solving the problem by growing your character. We will address this in the "Quitting" subchapter below.

QUITTING

You should never quit. You should not quit because it damages yourself and it damages all of those who look up to you.

Let's first focus on yourself. You have thrust yourself into a situation that is incredibly tough and challenging that most people will never be able to face let alone understand. You see, most people go through life on autopilot and float. Am I saying most people have easy lives and are never faced with difficult challenges? No. This is a prerequisite to being a human. What I am saying is that most people are met with a challenge and let it impact them negatively for the rest of their lives. They face challenges brought upon them by the nature of life, kinda fumble through it with copious amounts of complaining and self-pity, and just emerge on the other side a little worse for wear. They don't conquer the problem nor become an expert on the solution. Most people get beat around by life and just deal with it.

I always try to dive deep into people's lives and discover their fears and anxieties. It's one of my favorite pastimes. Oddly enough, I hear very similar stories. "My parents weren't really there for me growing up. This has made me struggle with anxiety, making me overall a generally anxious person." "My mother was always so critical of me. I have no self-confidence." "In elementary school, I was a chunkier kid and was made fun of. Now I have body image issues." These are all made-up stories but they have the exact same theme as the real stories I hear from friends and colleagues. Some uncontrollable problem of life reared its ugly head, inflicted mental and emotional damage, and then that's it. The person just takes that damage and accepts they are forever scarred by the new emotional and mental weakness. There is no battle against the emotional anguish or struggle, there is just taking the loss.

But here you are! In a space to battle back and overcome! To learn something new about life and use it positively. I could have easily quit volleyball. In fact, I was about to quit. However, I am so thankful that a lucky change in circumstance helped me stop myself from quitting. Because I didn't quit, I developed a new philosophy in life and have become a much stronger person. If I quit, I would have become scarred by my overall situation at Ship Weight instead of using it to develop my character. I highly doubt I would have gotten to play professionally because I never would have developed my philosophy to become a better player mentally (and at that level, you have to be strong mentally). I would have always been weak and struggled with athletic performance anxiety. In short, battling through such a difficult challenge presented to me by Ship Weight and coming out victorious was so impactful in my life that I'm scared to think about the person I would have become if I ended up quitting.

So don't quit. Don't end up like the majority of the world - sad, depressed, and lamenting their past traumas. Don't end up scarred and mentally weak, accepting the next whooping life brings upon you. Don't just autopilot and fade into the background of life. Don't avoid triumph over major problems. Don't just accept who you are and accept all of your problems. Battle back and invent! Use RARP. Hell, use RARP to develop your own philosophy. Become a stronger person. Eliminate your weaknesses. Become mentally unbreakable and the person you want to be. Become the main character. Become the hero of the world.

Speaking of becoming the hero of the world, think about what quitting does to the people that look up to you. If you are playing a collegiate sport, someone from your past is looking up to you, I guarantee it. When you played in high school, or when you played in an intramural team, or when you played pickup with your dad at the local park, you met someone that was inspired by you. Whether it be your skill or your dedication to the sport, someone admires you. Even if you are a walk-on and the worst player on the team, someone somewhere is going, "remember that kid who played with me at this place. He plays at *insert the school you go to that you think is garbage.* That's so cool." I'll never forget about the time my Dad told me his friend's son, who was a couple of years younger than me, used to watch me play and model his defense after me. He would watch film of himself and be critical of his missed digs because he "knew that Ryan would make those digs."

It's funny how we view ourselves. In college, I viewed my volleyball career as a bit disappointing. Before developing RARP, I saw myself as this pity player who only went in the game because the starter got suspended. Meanwhile, people who knew me were so proud that I was even there. They were amazed I was following my passion and playing at the Division I level.

Again, you have the choice. You can be the hero and inspire people. Even if you don't start a single minute, people are looking up to you, wanting to be you, are amazed by you, and are in awe of your dedication to your sport and your achievements. You can be the light for people and allow them to use you as a beacon of hope. You can give people the opportunity to say "I want to play my sport just like you when I get to college."

The other option is the rejection of being the hero. This option lets people down and reiterates the sad excuse that life is hard and crushing. Anyone that flies too high will be pulled back down, steamed rolled, and reduced to an autopiloting background character. People no longer can look to you for inspiration and instead will just be reminded of the reality of life's drudgeries. "Remember that kid that made it and played in college? That was amazing. I heard he quit and is not doing much with his life... like the rest of us."

It's not like you're quitting to pursue an even harder challenge to become a stronger hero for those that look up to you. You're quitting to make your life easier for the now. You're taking the easier route, pursuing a road of mental weakness for the future, and abandoning your heroic responsibility so you can fade into the background of stagnancy, complacency, and self-loathing.

Don't transfer or quit because the challenge is too difficult or because you're momentarily unhappy. Battle through the challenge and you'll thank yourself in the future.

CHAPTER 15

How To Deal With Your Emotions

Throughout the book, I've encouraged you to implement RARP, identify and accept things you cannot control, and basically come to peace with that. You now know how to deal with many common and difficult situations. To be a robot, you really have to have your emotions in check and be the master of them.

When your coach is yelling at you, you feel sad and scared but RARP tells you to be emotionless and disconnected from your body. When your teammate is The Coacher you get extremely angry but RARP tells you to be unbothered. When you feel the urge to change the program and self-promote, RARP tells you to disobey your feelings and be a pawn.

How can you become the master of your emotions?

The guide to mastering anything is practice. Before you practice, however, you must understand what emotions are and how to view them.

YOUR FEELINGS ARE NOT VALID

What are emotions? Emotions are tools that kept the human species alive during caveman days. That is all. It is as simple as that. Anger was great for the caveman because he got his adrenaline rushing so he could fight off a foe. Anxiety was great for the caveman so he could be on alert and prevent being snuck up on by a foe. Embarrassment helped prevent the caveman from being ostracized by his peers whom he counted on for survival. Jealousy empowered the caveman to fight for his mate to reproduce. Love drew the caveman to mate and reproduce. Emotions, these biological triggers, are excellent at keeping you alive, especially when in danger. Unfortunately, they suck at helping us navigate our world today. When you are at your college you are not in constant danger. You are not trying to survive in the wilderness or fight a jaguar. Therefore, emotions do not apply to your situation most of the time. In other words, all humans are using ancient tools to solve modern problems and these tools aren't great.

These emotions and feelings just don't work today. Is it beneficial to have sudden and strong urges to fight your coach when you are angry because he tells you that you suck at your sport? No. Is it beneficial to constantly be on alert when you are anxious so you can prevent your fellow students from sneaking up and attacking you? No. Is it beneficial to be flooded with adrenaline and kicked into fight or flight mode when you are embarrassed because you told a bad joke at a party? No. Is it beneficial to be encouraged to confront or attack a stranger when you are jealous because he is talking to the cute girl you had your eye on in the frat basement? No. See how these emotional responses don't work for your environment?

Therefore, YOUR FEELINGS ARE NOT VALID. As shocking as that may sound, it is the truth. I do not know who invented the belief that all feelings are valid. I think this is the most detrimental belief a person can have, not just in college but in life.

RUN BY YOUR FEELINGS

Allowing yourself to believe that all of your feelings are valid can be very damaging. If all of your feelings are valid, that means your feelings are infallible. Thus, your feelings can never be wrong. This means that your feelings are perfectly trustworthy and it only makes sense that you venture in life based on your feelings. You follow your feelings, you follow your heart, and you let them guide you into making the correct decision. If you have this line of logic you are doomed and must abort from this thinking at all costs.

As described before, your feelings are fake. They do not resemble reality or the truth. People that are run by their feelings are normally undisciplined, mentally weak, make terrible decisions, feel everything is out of their control, and end up being background characters in their own lives. They want to change jobs but are fearful, so they trust their fear and stay. They want to say a witty joke but feel awkward, cringey, or embarrassed, so they lay low and don't say anything. They feel anger at the slightest inconvenience so they wallow in it for the whole day. They are saddened by something traumatizing from their past and never overcome it and become chronically depressed. They stick around in terrible relationships because they feel love. They feel resentful for being slighted so they hold a grudge forever. They do absolutely nothing when they feel lazy. They are most likely addicted to nicotine because it makes them feel happy and calm when they smoke. When they have emotional overload and there are too many feelings they drink to numb everything. When they go through a break up they stay devastated for months and months and months. They act on every emotion and never keep them in check. Why would they? Their feelings are valid. Their feelings *are the truth*.

RUNNING YOUR FEELINGS

When your feelings are valid you don't challenge them. You don't question them. They are unchangeable and uncontrollable. If you feel intense sadness - that's it. There's no hope. Your only solution is death, time, drugs, or alcohol. Obviously, you do not want to be in this situation. You want to control your feelings instead of allowing them to control you. How can you do this?

I have a five-step procedure for any time you feel any negative emotion to help you become the master of your emotions.

STEP 1: *Define Your Emotion*

Whenever you feel a negative emotion, you need to stop and question it. This means any time you feel a negative emotion no matter where you are it *must* be questioned. The first step you need to do is to ask yourself, "what am I feeling?" Your job is to find specific words that define exactly how you are feeling. The words must be exact. They cannot be all-inclusive words like "overwhelmed." Then, store these words in your memory or write them down. Sometimes it is really easy and you feel one emotion. I feel sad. Done. Other times it's a strange mix of emotions that you have to sort out.

Let's use this example throughout the guide. You are chilling in bed and a wave of negative emotions flows over you right before you fall asleep. You sit up and feel it deep in your stomach. You ask yourself "what am I feeling?" You search for the exact descriptor that does your feelings justice. You conclude that you exactly feel annoyed, betrayed, and angered.

STEP 2: *Determine The Origin*

Once you have exactly picked out the emotions you feel, you have to ask yourself "where did this come from?" You must find out what event has caused you emotional turmoil. Sometimes the event happened five minutes ago. Sometimes the event happened eight years ago.

Continuing with the example, you determine that the feelings of annoyance, betrayal, and anger came from an event at practice. You arrived one minute late to practice earlier today and your teammate HeLd YoU AcCoUnTaBlE by yelling at you to show up on time.

STEP 3: Analyze The Why

Now that you have determined the event, you have to dig deep and ask yourself why you feel the way you do. The answer cannot be the event. You must exactly define why you fundamentally are negatively impacted. Did the event conflict with your view of life? Did the event stir up past traumas? Did the event interfere with your ego? Keep asking yourself questions. You must analyze each emotion.

Continuing with the example, you analyze your three emotions.

Why do you feel annoyed? You determine the annoyance stems from the fact that you have been working on showing up earlier to practice yet still failed. You find your lack of immediate progress annoying because you have higher standards for yourself.

Why do you feel betrayed? You determine the betrayal stems from your understanding of a teammate. You view teammates as companions above all else. Instead of welcoming you to practice as a friend, your teammate decided to abandon your friendship and become your coach, leaving you feeling betrayed.

Why do you feel anger? You determine the anger stems from your understanding of a team. You view a team as a group of all equals and are angered that someone is trying to rise above the rest, therefore forcing inequality. The fact that someone is trying to obtain power over you, angers you.

STEP 4: Detach From Your Emotions

Now you understand what real emotional analysis looks like. From this point, you must detach from your emotions. To do this, you must explain why your emotional distress is warranted in caveman days, but is not in today's society. In other words, you are explaining why these emotions are not real and that they are just tricks to help you survive in scenarios that are not happening. You are stepping outside of yourself and noting that your own emotions are simply biological triggers that are unimportant.

With the example, let's start with annoyance. You felt annoyed because you are not living up to the standards you set for yourself in terms of tardiness. Back in caveman days, the standard was being alive and reproducing. So if a caveman underperformed in that regard, it meant he was dead. Certainly, some sort of negative feeling like annoyance should be conjured up to alert the caveman if he falls below the expectation so he won't die. Will you die if you fail to show up on time to practice? No. So the biological triggers that come with annoyance are unwarranted.

You felt betrayed because your teammate momentarily abandoned your friendship. Back in the caveman days, if the caveman lost a friend, his chances of survival decreased exponentially. Not only that, a past friend can easily turn into an enemy. It makes sense for feelings of betrayal to invoke a sense of danger because the caveman needs to either protect himself from a new foe or take action to increase his chances of survival. If you lose a friend or a friend is mean to you, are you in danger of dying? No. So the biological triggers that come with betrayal are unwarranted.

Finally, you feel anger because an equal is trying to obtain power over you. In caveman days, maybe this was a major problem because if the caveman fell to the bottom of the pecking order, he would be deprived of food and die. If you become the weakest member on the team are you going to die? No. So the biological triggers, like the rush of adrenaline, that come with anger are unwarranted.

STEP 5: Logic It Out

At this point, you have felt emotions, defined them precisely, determined where the feelings came from, analyzed why the event disturbs you on a fundamental level of your being, and determined that the emotions are drummed up to keep you alive and do not represent reality. Finally, you must logic out what you should do to calm the negative emotion. In other words, you must logically solve it. In order to solve the emotion, you must coax yourself back into homeostasis. You must tell yourself, "yeah, I feel anger but the emotion is just a dumb biological trigger. The truth is... (insert truth here)." When completing Step 5, the truth is comprised of two objective elements.

The first part of the truth is the reality. Emotions are archaic but very convincing. The brain will conjure up all of these doubts and scenarios to try to prepare you and help you survive but, most of the time, the reality is the opposite of what your emotions are telling you. When you tell a bad joke your feelings give you an encompassing sense of panic, the feeling that you're in danger, and the feeling to run. The reality is that you are perfectly safe in a house with your friends. When you are pulled from the game, your feelings tell you to be seething in anger and to fight someone. The reality is that you were simply moved several feet from the action of a *game that does not matter.* The outcome doesn't matter, the game doesn't matter, none of it matters. You were simply instructed to move to a different space on earth. You are still healthy and perfectly safe.

The other half of the truth is the ideal. This is the most important part. You understand your feeling is just an archaic emotional trigger. You understand the reality of your situation and that you are not in danger. Now what? If your emotion was a final boss in a video game, your ideal for yourself is the finishing blow. The commitment to the ideal version of yourself is what must drive your actions. For me, my ideal version of myself in life, outside of sports, is a hero from a fairytale. I always want to be the hero. Once I get to this point in the process, I ask myself "what would a hero do" and then I do it. This is the most beautiful part of the process because you are about to make a decision that is purely rooted in logic and your ideal, unswayed by emotion. For our scenario, when we are in the world of collegiate sports, guess what your ideal is? Yep. It's to be a robot. You must ask yourself, "what would a robot do?" Then, you must act based on the teachings of RARP.

Let's finish the example. For all three of your emotions, you step back and look at the reality of the situation. You remove all social context. You conclude that you are showing up to an event that's just for fun to play a game that's just for fun, at a time that was arbitrarily defined. You showed up late to the arbitrary time to play an invented game. The reality of the situation is that you are safe at school, not in danger at all, and playing your sport for your own human entertainment.

You now think about your ideal. What would a robot do in response to showing up late? A robot would understand that showing up on time is a skill you are practicing so the probability of success for showing up on time will be lower than the ideal. In order to increase the probability of successful completion of the skill to show up on time, you must practice. In order to practice, you must change something about your life. To help you practice you immediately set three alarms to go off well before practice starts so you can depart even earlier than before.

What would a robot do in response to being betrayed by a friend/ teammate? A robot would conclude that the teammate's actions are out of its control and is unbothered. A bot allows this strange outside force of a teammate randomly self-promoting and concludes that it is a glitch in the team system. It ignores the absurdity of the situation but tries to grasp any value out of the words. It understands that showing up late is not only bad for itself but also bad for the team. It concludes it has already set up a system to try to increase the probability of success (the alarms it just set) and continues to do its next task.

What would a robot do in response to being challenged in a power hierarchy? A robot does not even know what that is. A robot is just trained to do its job. It will ignore any sense of power change because it concludes that it does not affect its probabilities of success at performing its actions of the sport. The robot moves to its next action.

A FINAL NOTE

My five-step procedure will not instantly cure you of negative emotions. If it were that easy, and implementing my technique was that simple, I would be the most famous person in the world. Many negative feelings linger and reoccur. But the goal is to create a logic pattern in your brain to come to peace with the emotion. Maybe the first time you feel a negative emotion it takes you two hours to get from step 1 to step 5. But after practicing it and repeating the process and thinking of exact words like in the example, that process will get faster. Then when you feel a negative emotion you can come to peace with it in ten seconds as opposed to doing nothing and allowing it to linger on for hours, days, months, years, and ultimately become life-shatteringly devastated by it.

You may ask, "if my emotions are not the end all truth, what is my foundation for living life?" This is an excellent question. If the goal in life is not to simply listen to your emotions, if it's not to avoid the sad/hard things and do the happy/easy things, what is the goal? Step 5 from above has the answer. The goal of life is to get ever closer to your ideal version of yourself, so you can be proud of who you are. You have to overcome your emotions to fulfill the duty of moving toward your ideal. That is why you must constantly overcome emotions of laziness to work out or do homework, feelings of sadness or purposelessness to support your friends and family, and feelings of anger to be mature. You must overcome your emotions, which a lot of times fight directly against your goal, to get closer to the ideal version of yourself. If you become the passenger to your emotions and purely listen to them, you risk falling into the saddest scenario a human can adore - at the end of one's life, looking back and being dissatisfied.

Even though emotions are archaic, they are not entirely useless. They are excellent at telling you something is wrong. However, it's not enough to just feel emotions and take them as truth. Follow my five-step process, become a detective, scrutinize your feelings, learn about yourself, find a solution, and grow as a person.

CHAPTER 16

Toxic Femininity

After reading the previous chapter you might be wondering why I am assaulting emotions. Why am I trying to downplay the value of your emotions? Why am I encouraging you to value your ideal version of yourself and your dreams over your emotions? Why am I telling you to scrutinize your emotions? There are two reasons.

The first reason has already been described. In order to implement RARP and become a robot you must become a master of your emotions. Since we cannot simply turn off our emotions, we must have a strategy for overcoming them. That is why I wrote the subchapter "Running Your Feelings."

The other reason is that I believe the current remedy for the student-athlete mental health crisis is flawed. I believe that toxic femininity is being promoted as a solution for the mental struggle of student-athletes.

Allow me to first explain the differences and similarities between toxic masculinity and toxic femininity by using the scale below. Toxic masculinity and toxic femininity are very broad and vague topics. I will only focus on the concept of how they affect dealing with your emotions.

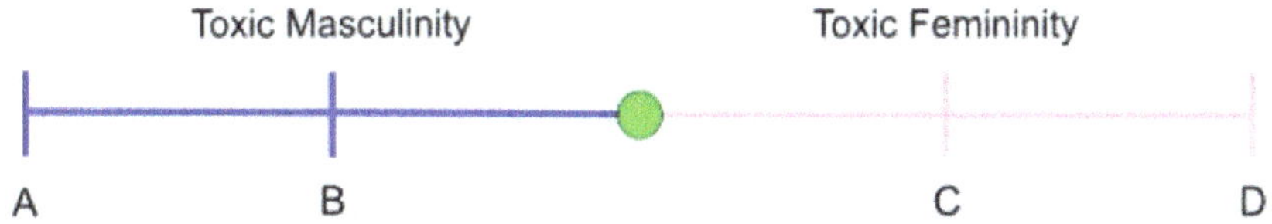

Looking at the graph, you want to be at the green dot. The green dot represents mental peace. On the left side of the scale, the blue part, we have toxic masculinity. On the right side of the scale, the pink part, we have toxic femininity.

First, we must analyze points A and D. These two points represent the failure to analyze your emotions.

You are probably familiar with point A, as toxic masculinity has grown to be a popular buzzword in society. At point A, you refuse to admit that your feelings have any validity and completely ignore them. You can't even accept the possibility that you are experiencing a negative emotion. For example, a person who is operating at point A will feel sadness and won't admit it. He will pretend the feeling does not exist.

At point D, you refuse to admit that your feelings are fallible and completely accept them. You can't even accept the possibility that your emotions might be unwarranted and thus you feel totally justified to act them out. For example, a person who is operating at point D will feel sadness and immediately cry no matter what setting he is in and no matter how trivial the event is that caused the sadness.

Notice how point A and point D are actually the same concept. Completely rejecting and completely accepting your emotions are both actions that decline the analysis of your emotions.

Working in, away from toxicity and toward peace, we have points B and C. These two points represent the admittance that you can analyze your emotions but the rejection that you can analyze your perception of reality. Analyzing your perception of reality is the idea of questioning if your interpretation of the truth matches the actual truth.

At point B, you admit you are feeling a negative emotion. However, you do not care why or how that emotion originated. To solve the new and annoying negative emotion, you just truck through, performing zero analysis of reality. For example, a person who is operating at point B will feel sadness and simply tell himself, "let's take our mind off of it and just be happy."

At point C, you admit that emotions are fallible and they should not always dictate how you behave. However, you conclude that all feelings are justified and it doesn't matter how you became sad. The only way back to peace is to suffer through the mental dissonance, performing zero analysis of reality. For example, a person who is operating at point C will feel sadness from an event and will not check his expectations for the event or perception of reality of the event to see if the feeling is justified. He will just suffer through the pain of the emotion until time heals the wound.

Point C is a bit complex so allow me to give another example. Let's say I expect my girlfriend to surprise me with flowers today because I casually mentioned I liked flowers yesterday. When my girlfriend doesn't bring me flowers I am devastated. I understand it is not appropriate to lash out at my girlfriend and express my sadness. But, I never question if my expectation for flowers is justified. I never question the perception of reality that my girlfriend *should have* brought me flowers. I remain sad, even though it was my own faulty interpretation of reality that caused my sadness, and remain sad until the feeling naturally wears off.

In the past, I believe we had a collegiate athlete environment that was on the left side of the scale and was one of toxic masculinity. This environment contained the detrimental concepts of points A and B. Emotions were disregarded and coaches told their athletes to "suck it up and get back out there" when struggling with mental health issues. Clearly, this is not valuable advice because it does not provide any long-term solutions to mental health struggles and we have moved away from this environment.

Unfortunately, I believe we have overcorrected in the collegiate athlete world to the right side of the scale and have created an environment of toxic femininity. This environment contains the detrimental concepts of points C and D. Emotions are infallible and coaches tell their athletes that "your feelings and experiences are valid." This is not valuable advice for the same reason. It does not provide any long-term solutions.

The main offender that is keeping student-athletes in the toxic feminine environment is the concept that your feelings, emotions, perceptions of reality, and experiences are always valid. I'm sure you have heard it before.

"Your feelings are always valid."
"You're valid to feel that way."
"Your experience is valid."
"Who are you to invalidate his feelings?!"
"Who are you to invalidate his experience?!"

When you tell someone that his feelings and experiences are always valid, you remove the ability to scrutinize them. If something is always valid and cannot be scrutinized, it gets mistaken for the truth. This means there is nothing you can do when you have negative emotions. The truth can never be altered, and if your interpretation of reality and feelings are the truth, they cannot be altered either. You are completely locked, and the only thing you can do is ride out the mental anguish. Like I said before, the only remedies you can receive at this point are death, time, drugs, alcohol, and comfort from others. None of these remedies solve your mental strife nor do they offer you mental defense against future difficult situations.

This is why I made an effort in the previous chapter to lower the value of your emotions. I am fighting against these widely accepted concepts of toxic femininity. I want you to understand that your emotions do not have to dictate your life.

I want you to understand that in order to implement RARP you have to let go of toxic femininity and be able to scrutinize your perception of reality and your emotions.

CHAPTER 17

How To Deal With The Loose Ends

Upon writing this book, I struggled to find a home for the advice I had for problems that were not large enough to warrant their own chapter. How to deal with these "loose ends" can mostly be inferred using your knowledge of RARP. Nonetheless, according to my friends and me, these problems are common challenges faced in a collegiate athlete's journey and you will most likely have to deal with most of them.

HOW TO DEAL WITH BEING INJURED

Your robot body is broken! That is frustrating for sure. There are three types of injuries. There is an injury that changes nothing, an injury that changes your play, and an injury that ends your play.

First, and most commonly, you have an injury that changes nothing. You will heal soon and you'll be exactly back to normal. Maybe soon means two days, two weeks, or two months. During this time, implement RARP. You cannot control that you are injured. There is no magical cure. You can stretch, use the stim machine, ice it, cup it, do the hokey pokey, whatever. Time is the real cure for your common injury and you cannot speed up time. It is completely out of your control. Instead of being sad or angry over something that cannot be changed, accept your injured state of being, and find out your temporary new role for the team. If your new role at practice is to do stats, sit there and watch, or not show up to practice at all, accept it and don't let it ruin your college time. When you look back you don't want to think, "that two-month period when I was hurt was miserable and I was depressed." Are you going to be depressed every time you get hurt? You want to look back and think, "it was unfortunate that I was injured. But during that time I killed it at school and learned how to solve a Rubik's Cube."

Second, and more frustrating, you have an injury that changes your play. Let's say you have to get surgery and can no longer jump as high as you could before. You work on it and improve it the best you can to get it close to what it once was but it's not quite the same. At this point, a lot of people simply quit. You'll meet these people five years out of college and they'll say something like "I was so good until I got hurt and you should've seen me back when yada yada yada." Every athlete gets hurt; the older you get, the more injuries you have to deal with. The best athletes adapt and develop new, sometimes even better styles of play. The amount of times I've lost tournaments to older men who struggle to move is astonishing. They've adapted with impeccable shot refinement and defensive reading.

If you find your body has changed after an injury you must implement RARP and accept your new form. Embrace that you must play slightly differently and strategize. Invent and be creative. What must you do differently with your new form? My volleyball partner, Jake, once tore a ligament in his right thumb during a tournament. We won that same tournament with a one-handed, lefty, solo block by Jake. Jake accepted the status of his thumb and adapted. You can too.

Finally, the saddest, you suffer an injury that ends your play. Maybe your body really becomes permanently damaged and you simply have constant pain when you play. You've gotten surgery, and you've tried everything you could to return, but nothing has worked. You must implement RARP. Understand that you cannot control that you are injured. What you can control is how well you do in the mental battle that ensues. Are you going to lament the fact that you are injured for the rest of your life, always carrying this burden of sadness? Or are you going to find a new adventure, continue your destiny for greatness, and move toward your ideal?

For a final note, the last thing you want to do is continue playing through an injury or delay surgery to prolong your college career. Ten years from now you're not going to really remember much about the matches. You'll remember the impactful memories (hopefully good), and your character will be forever changed (hopefully for the better), but you won't remember the specifics. Hell, I'm two years out and I have difficulty remembering a single specific play from a collegiate match. However, if you are having health issues later in life, you certainly will remember back in college when you didn't rest when injured or when you put off surgery to play some game that doesn't even matter. Don't play when your body needs a break and don't allow anyone to force you to play when you know your body needs to heal.

HOW TO DEAL WITH PLAYING ON A SHORT LEASH

When you implement RARP you identify what you can and cannot control. Your coach subbing you out is completely out of your control. Your coach will come up with millions of reasons to support his case for subbing you out. All of these reasons cannot mask the truth that your coach is probably just reacting on a biased and unsubstantiated gut feeling.

The worst thing you can do is believe "well, if I just play extremely well or perfectly, then the coach will have no reason to take me out of the game and I'll remain in." This logic is doubly faulted. First, to reiterate, your coach can sub you out even when you're playing perfectly for infinitely many dumb reasons. You cannot prevent or be one step ahead of illogical bias. Secondly, and more importantly, when you think like this, you pull yourself out of RARPing. You are completely throwing away the truth behind the probabilities of success and believe that you can somehow play at a 100% success rate. Now, when you make an error, you become angry with yourself, flustered, and annoyed that you are not "performing at your best." You stop thinking about the opponent and strategizing and become consumed by the fear of being pulled. Instead, when you make an error like described previously, you should RARP, accept your probabilities of success for that game, and constantly be critically thinking about the opponent so you can re-strategize.

By believing you can control whether you are pulled or not, you are creating a self-fulfilling prophecy of failure simply because you are not RARPing.

So, what should you do? Remember that you are a pawn. It is not about you, it is not about your playtime, and it is your coach's team. It is all completely out of your control. You just show up and follow orders. If your coach wants to play you for a single point then so be it. If his reason for doing so is because a leprechaun told him to while he was sleeping, so be it. Do what you are told, be proud that you are in a system that others dream about being in, work on your probabilities of success at practice and the off-season, chase the ideal version of yourself, and have fun. You're in college. Don't waste it being sad about something completely out of your control.

HOW TO DEAL WITH THE YIPS

Players who claim they have the yips say they randomly can no longer perform a practiced action. All of a sudden and out of nowhere they can no longer shoot anywhere close to the basket, pitch a strike if their life depended on it, or dribble in a straight line toward the goal. The yips are like an invisible disease. Catching the disease is completely random and mysterious. It short-circuits your brain in some unknown way. How to cure yourself of the disease is equally unknown. Some players are blessed and the yips go away on their own, while other players never recover.

This is wrong. The yips are not real.

The yips can easily be disproven. Why would yips only exist for your sport and not for other skills? If the yips were real, then everyone would randomly be unable to do any practiced action, not just in sports. Why don't you catch the yips for things like brushing your teeth, drinking water, jogging, walking up the stairs, writing with a pen, typing on a computer, or other practiced actions?

The reason you don't catch the yips for actions outside of your sport is because you don't believe in the yips for these scenarios. So why do you believe in the yips for scenarios in your sport? Throwing, setting, or kicking a ball is just like any other practiced action.

Let's say I tripped up the stairs three times on one trek. What would you think if I told you that I must've caught the stair yips? What would you think if I told you my solution for overcoming the stair yips was to stop psyching myself out, stop being so nervous, clear my mind, focus more, relax, or distract myself by thinking about butterflies on each step?

You would think I'm a lunatic.

You would probably just tell me something like, "Hey Ryan, you're just hitting your right foot a couple of times because you are not clearing the height of every step. To fix this, just lift your leg higher."

In the scenario, your advice to me is a tangible solution while my line of thinking with the stair yips is an intangible solution. You want to implement RARP, view your body as a machine, and strictly think about physical solutions to errors in your sport. I advise this because mental solutions are too abstract and nearly unsolvable.

Let's say you're not quite on board yet with the idea of strictly finding physical solutions. Let's say you believe that the solutions of not psyching yourself out, removing nerves, clearing your mind, focusing more, becoming more relaxed, or distracting yourself are good solutions to overcoming the yips. How do you implement these solutions?

How do you stop psyching yourself out? How do you become less nervous? How do you clear your mind? Do you have to think less? What does it mean to think less? How do you think less? Can you measure how much you are thinking? Is that measured in thoughts per second? What does it mean to focus more? What do you need to focus more on? Were you not focusing previously? How can you measure the amount of focus you are giving? How do you become more relaxed?

How can you feel looser? How do you effectively distract yourself? How do you know you have distracted yourself?

Do you see how these questions are nearly impossible to answer and deal with concepts that are uncontrollable? Sure, you can do breathing exercises, practice visualization, tighten and then loosen your muscles, and do other sports psychology tricks. But, to me, these are band-aids over bullet holes. The real solution lies in fundamentally changing your philosophy and perception about the concept of what an athlete is and what errors are. The real solution is believing that your mind is separate from your robot body and no matter how you feel or what you think, it's your robot body performing the actions. The real solution lies in finding physical adjustments to your robot body because those adjustments are tangible and affect the real world. Correcting your robot's angle, force, or position, directly affects the physical world because you are making changes to reality. Correcting your mind's clarity level does not affect the physical world because you are just making changes to your perception of reality.

Believing in the yips is just a perception of reality and your perception of reality dictates your explanation for errors. If you believe in astrology and you miss three shots in a row, you conclude it's because you're a Capricorn, the stars aren't aligned, and there's nothing you can do. If you believe you're a robot, you conclude it's because of an exact physical reason, you identify that physical reason, and you practice fixing it.

Remember the chapter Toxic Femininity. You must scrutinize your perception of reality. Your perception of reality is not always valid. You can alter your perception of reality. You can choose your perception of reality. You can choose to not believe in astrology. You can choose to not believe in the yips. You can choose to believe that you will be able to perform despite your thoughts and emotions. Your emotions do not have all-consuming power over you. You have control.

Adjust your perception of reality, focus on things you can control like physical solutions to errors, and you will find mental peace.

HOW TO DEAL WITH TEAMMATES YOU DISLIKE

The probability of you liking everyone on your team is basically zero. There are just too many people on your team now. It's not like in high school or club where you had three subs on the team. You now have 17 subs. The environment becomes even more difficult because you are dealing with people that are trying to be adults but do not have the experience to do so (the natural path of life). For many of your teammates, including you, this is the first real challenge to your mental state and soul. This may be the first time you envisioned something epic and had to face the reality that the vision may be unobtainable in the time you are given. This is the first time you and your teammates are not the starters. You have been thrust into an environment where people are unequipped to handle tough mental battles without devolving, whining, crying, breaking down, and becoming emotionally overtaken. And guess what? You're one of them. If you think you are the exception, you are super ultra infinitely wrong.

When people who are unequipped to handle emotional turmoil meet emotional turmoil, it gets scary, fast. I've known *several* teammates who have cut themselves and had suicidal thoughts. I've had many teammates, including me, become ghosts of themselves, depressed, irrationally angry, devoid of purpose, disconnected from their origin, and completely lost. Other teammates I knew became irrational bullies, snarky, merciless, and almost evil as they spiraled further and further out of control.

What can you do with these teammates? Understand that whatever negativity they impose onto you, most of the time it's the out-of-control shrapnel from the battle of chaos they are going through in their heads. Hopefully, they will come out with emotional armor better equipped for life. Some won't.

You do not have to like all of your teammates. Nor do you have to hang out with any of your teammates. As long as you implement RARP on the court, you are guaranteed to be a good teammate that ensures you are doing your job well. Understand that not everyone is implementing

RARP. If you are receiving manipulative and negative feedback from your teammate, disassociate from yourself, let your teammate be toxic to your robot body, and try to see if there is any valuable information from your teammate's wild expression of their chaotic emotions.

There is an incredible quote about romance that I adore. It is, "everyone is trying to find the one but no one is trying to become the one." In other words, no one is trying to become an excellent, emotionally sound person in order to attract other people of the same caliber. The same applies to your scenario. You can read the above text and think highly of yourself that you are the outcast of your team and that they are just emotionally out of control. You're not like that. You're above all that. Are you sure?

Remember, a lot of my team hated me. I attempted to manhandle the culture of the team and correct it into something different. Was I the savior who wanted to save the team culture from objectively bad seniority, hazing, and bullying to give us a better chance of winning? Or, was I the naive fool who was thrust into a new culture and wanted to force it and everyone else into the type of culture I wanted? Am I a savior or just selfish? Probably a little of both.

It is important to analyze yourself this way. You know which teammates you dislike, but are you the teammate to be disliked? Are you emotionally out of control just with a pompous false belief that you are in control? Do you constantly lament your situation? Do you wish your team culture was different? Have you outwardly expressed negative emotions (sadness, anger, frustration, snarkiness, impatience) to your teammates? Are you quick to anger or easily devastated? Is everything a huge deal? Do you act blindly on your emotions? Are you a bit illogical?

Maybe it's you.

You have room to grow. Just make sure you keep trying to develop yourself, okay? I believe in you.

The Conclusion: Nihilism Vs Heroism

You've made it to the end. Congratulations. I've shared a lot of unconventional and controversial wisdom with you. It is now your time to decide what to do with this information. The way I see it you can do three things with this book.

First, you can completely disregard everything I've said and write me off as a crazy wingnut who knows nothing. If that is the case I wish you the best of luck. I hope you come up with an even better philosophy than mine. Even if it does not apply to you now (you're the starter all four years, you have a great coach, you perfectly get along with your team, and you have no problems), my book may apply to you in the future. Remember this advice does not only apply to collegiate athletics, it applies to life. Maybe just one thing I've said can come in handy for the next challenge life throws your way.

The second thing, and by far the absolute worst thing, is you can become completely nihilistic and uncaring. It is really easy to take all of the information I've given you in this book and simply give up. Your coach sucks, your feelings don't matter, you're just a pawn, you have no power, you're burnt out, you're disappointed in your team culture, and you're tired. It is easy to logic out, "well, if this is my scenario then what is the point?" It is easy to think that there is no point to continue, there is no point to play a game that doesn't matter, and there is *no purpose.*

At any point in life, if you feel completely nihilistic and cannot find a purpose in anything, you are in a very bad place and need to escape that mindset at all costs. As I stated earlier in the book, humans need purpose as much as they need air and water. If you conclude there is no purpose, you are dying internally. Nihilism really is a self-fulfilling prophecy to a sad life. You can't find purpose in anything and are sad, so you don't do anything because there is no point, making your life even more sad and purposeless. Do not let yourself fall for the trap that playing your sport is pointless, collegiate sports are pointless, or life is pointless.

The third thing you can do is take all of my philosophies, accept them, and become the hero of your situation. You can pull your shoulders back, keep your head high, step into the arena of collegiate athletics, grapple with your adventure, make companions, make memories, fight the lows, relish in the highs, work toward your ideal version of yourself and your life, and achieve greatness. Even if it is not exactly what you wanted, you don't get to start, or whatever; you are completing a mission with great honor. You are completing the mission to finish your dream of being a collegiate athlete and develop yourself as a person to better the people around you and therefore the world. You can step up and accept the challenge of collegiate athletics, the challenge of life, get outside of your comfort zone, and implement a new philosophy, RARP.

As long as you keep fighting, keep internally reflecting, keep implementing RARP, and keep trying to become a better person and a better athlete, you'll come out the other side an adult one step closer to your ultimate form, your ideal.

Good luck player.

Ryan Alu, a volleyball player out of Pennsylvania, competed at a Division I level from the years 2017-2020 at his undergraduate institution. Upon graduating with degrees in computer science, math, and cyber security, Ryan went on to obtain his master's degree in computer science at Dartmouth College in New Hampshire (2021-2023).

It was at Dartmouth where Ryan founded his company, Idealism Towers, and initiated Project Save Collegiate Athletes. His motivation to start the company and write his book stemmed from his experience volunteering with the Dartmouth Women's Varsity Volleyball Team. Noticing that the players were experiencing the same hardships, challenges, and mental struggles as Ryan during his time as a student-athlete, he felt compelled to offer advice.

With his interest in philosophy and experience as a collegiate athlete, combined with the lessons learned from playing professionally for the National Volleyball Association (2020-2023), Ryan crafted the ultimate guide to surviving collegiate athletics with his book, Project Save Collegiate Athletes.

Ryan's goal is to cure the ailing minds of college athletes and alleviate the nationwide student-athlete mental health epidemic.

www.ingramcontent.com/pod-product-compliance
Lightning Source LLC
Chambersburg PA
CBHW071328140726
47996CB00005B/1872